MOVING TO INDEPENDENCE

A Support Worker's Guide To Preparing Individuals To Leave Supported Accommodation Such As Foster Care Or Prison

By

Eileen Williams

ISBN-13: 9781719869508

To Richard, who shared this journey with me.

CONTENTS

INTRODUCTION

There is a strong possibility that you are reading my book because you are in the unique position of preparing individuals for a move from supported living to independence. My ideas regarding this important change are contained within three Core Concepts, each one comprising of several related topics. Each Concept within the book stands alone and dipping in and out is the best way to work through it, however, you can go from beginning to end if this seems appropriate at the time. It is a good idea to make notes, not only of your own thoughts as you work, but also to keep track of where your clients are with the subjects discussed.

My suggestion is, keep things simple and informal; some of the ideas you will be working with might prove to be challenging for your clients so go gently and use your intuition. Before moving to independence is the very best time for this preparatory work to be done, you can ensure there is plenty of time for thinking and reflecting on the issues raised as well as appropriate support. For you too, approach your work mindfully, using patience and sincerity; you will be sharing the journey!

I was inspired to write this book through work I had done with young people and ex- offenders. For many years I was a foster carer, I worked at a project for homeless young people and at a probation hostel. The boy we had fostered eventually left us to move on to live independently with a minimum amount of support. However, it soon became clear that he had great difficulty in relating to his accommodation in any way. He didn't see any connection with it whatsoever and despite lots of encouragement and input from ourselves, it appeared that the thing holding him back from creating a proper home for himself was his inability to understand what he needed. He couldn't think clearly and logically about what would help him the most. I found the same with individuals at the project and at the hostel, they just couldn't relate their feelings and needs to the place where they lived, and they didn't understand that if they could, this would have been the very thing that would have helped them so much in creating some stability within their lives.

I believe passionately that a home provides a foundation in life, it is more than just somewhere to live. A real home is a sanctuary and an anchor for when life becomes unavoidably difficult and as you work with your clients, they will begin to move away from preconceived ideas of what independence will mean. You can help them develop a new frame of mind, bringing about a level of self-understanding that will enable them to create a safe space, built on strong foundations, designed specifically to meet their very individual needs.

Every client you work with is worthy of a home to feel safe in, not only from the outside world but also from internal fears and worries. By gently guiding individuals through my book the skills needed to provide a framework, both physically and psychologically, by which to live, can be learnt. This secure space will be safe enough to reliably withstand anxieties, insecurities or anger.

My book is not about interior design or soft furnishings. It will draw on positive past achievements as well as using hopes and ambitions for the future as tools to work with. The end result will be a home that is interwoven with these aspects and will reflect the whole personality of the client.

The Core Concepts are all linked by the main thread of the book which is to enable clients to understand themselves in such a way that they will be able to create a secure and permanent place to live. This will increase the chances of avoiding the sad outcome of so many people leaving supported living with research showing[1] that a high proportion of young people in particular become homeless within a relatively short period of time after becoming independent.

---

[1] *Understanding Youth: Perspectives, Identities and Practices*, p.298, Ed. Mary Jane Kehily

A Little Background

Most people's perception of home today is very different to what it was a few generations ago and there are lots of reasons why people are unable to connect with it as a place of stability and comfort. For these people, it is almost as if home has been removed from their line of vision and, evidence shows[2] that this lack of real connection with where they live can lead to unsociable behaviour which in turn brings about feelings of isolation and disassociation. In this frame of mind, individuals can go on to continue a cyclical life of petty crime and unruly behaviour with the use of drugs or alcohol often added to the mix.

So why are things so different today? Certainly over the last few decades our expectations have risen with regard to the material aspects of accommodation and general lifestyle. However, despite families sometimes being desperately poor, the quality of home life in the past, in terms of emotional stability, was very often far superior to what many families experience today.

A couple of generations ago, people lived very home-centred lives with clearly defined roles for everyone within that home. Because everybody knew where they were and what was expected of them, there was an amount of security, they felt safe enough to put down roots which then provided stability within the home and their lives. For everyone living there, this was their place to 'be'.

Clearly not all homes were wealthy, they were often very frugal and could involve a considerable amount of hard work to keep them running. Children would be expected to help

---

[2] Home Office Research Findings No. 127, p.2

with chores around the house as well as tending to chickens or the odd pig. However, despite sometimes being run in poverty, the quality of life, not the amount of material possessions, by today's standards, appears to have been incredibly high.[3]

These homes provided a strong sense of belonging, security and permanence.

These three things create the foundations of a home and when they are in place, the foundations of a life will naturally evolve, providing individuals with a world perspective that fits comfortably with who they are. This is the essence of what we all need in order to thrive; you have the opportunity to remind or teach your clients how to relate these things successfully to where they will ultimately live.

We can assume then that stable and secure homes are not dependent upon large sums of money being invested into them. Emotional value can be added by simply knowing what we need as individuals, and sometimes, even as mature adults, in the busy worlds we create for ourselves, we just don't get the time to really explore this. Vulnerable clients will probably not even think about this aspect of their accommodation, using my book you will be able to help them to do this.

Today, we all live much more mobile lifestyles and I would not suggest we readopt the past. What I do believe is that it is important to reclaim some of the attitudes and approaches to life that we once had. You will need to enable your clients to identify what will help them to create their own foundations. This will mean acknowledging the importance of their past life experiences as well as aspirations for the future, and then for individuals to accept and understand that the home can provide a holding environment that will facilitate personal development and growth where they are right now.

---

[3] *Homemaking as a Social Art*, p.1-3, Veronika Van Duin

CONCEPT ONE

YOUR HOME PROVIDES YOUR FOUNDATIONS TO LIFE AND IS YOUR SAFE HAVEN FROM THE WORLD

"Needs lower down in the hierarchy must be satisfied before we can attend to needs higher up."
Richard Gross commenting on Maslow's Hierarchy of Needs

1. 1 Foundations Within the Context of Home

The word 'foundation' means the basis of something which is usually much bigger. Whether a building, a principal or indeed a home, foundations are the first things that need to be put in place and they need to be strong.

Your clients will need to be encouraged to think about how they might begin to create some foundations for themselves within the context of a home; this will mean really beginning to understand themselves. You can help individuals to recognise some of the value of what has happened to them during their life so far, thus acknowledging that these experiences will all contribute to their character and personality. Past events are the cornerstones of life, and a home is where they can be integrated and put to good use.

Some of the reasons your clients may not value a home are within the list below and you can use these for discussions when opportunities arise, they may also have others of their own which will also need to be discussed.

- It is unusual for there to be an adult at home full time.

- Knowledge about running the home is not always passed down, more things are bought in and not made from scratch, for example food and clothing.

- Role models are not always available, different generations don't always share accommodation or live close by.

- The home is not used to its full potential, it isn't the place to 'just be'.

- There is no emotional attachment to home.

- People spend less time at home in creative pursuits, things they do spend time on while they are at home can often be solitary rather than social.

You can begin a discussion about how your clients see a home and what they expect from it. The list below clearly illustrates the view that many people share, you can use it to get a conversation going which will gently encourage consideration of what their expectations actually are.

Somewhere to eat and sleep.

Somewhere to invite friends.

A place to keep belongings.

Somewhere to watch TV and play games.

This view describes a basic home and this might well be all that your clients expect a home to provide. For many reasons, a home that could provide more than this has not entered their minds. Because of this then, when the move to independence happens it will be very difficult to put down the roots that are so badly needed. There will be no connection to the accommodation, your clients will see no more than four walls and a roof.

This viewpoint grossly undervalues the potential of a home and by accepting this without question and continuing this line of thought your clients could be seriously underrating their lives and themselves. As you work through my book you will be challenging this outlook and providing alternative approaches to the way a home can be viewed and valued.

It will be informative to explore the points below with your clients. You can look at the differences between a basic home and what a home created around your clients' needs might offer. When the time is right, ask your clients to write down the pros and cons on a large sheet of paper, allowing them to come up with as many answers as possible themselves. Ideally, everything on the list below should be discussed.

Basic Home – Disadvantages

- This kind of home might always feel like somebody else's because it hasn't got a personal stamp on it.

- Individuals will not want to spend time there because it feels cold or soulless.

- There will be no motivation to clean or look after it.

- It will be hard for individuals to become attached to this type of accommodation, the natural flow of emotions will be blocked and putting down roots will be very difficult.

Basic Home – Advantages

- It will be adequate.

Unique Home – Disadvantages

- Clients might need to move.

Unique Home – Advantages

- Home has become a safe place away from the outside world.

- It is a place to relax in.

- It contains the history and character of an individual, affirming who they are.

- Efforts that have been made are displayed, providing a sense of achievement and pride.

- Personality shines through, the home speaks about the individual and shows worthiness.

- If a move does need to happen, the essence of what has been created goes too, only the shell is left behind.

You can help your clients to understand that the differences between a basic home and a unique home are not about the cost, size, type, or the location of the building. The differences are all about how they feel when they are inside it.

Any home should provide for our basic needs, but if it only provides for these, it will be a cold and soulless place and will be ignoring our need for so much more. I believe the key to creating somewhere to live that will provide security, permanence and a sense of belonging is in knowing what we need and what we value as individuals in order for us to thrive, and then reflecting this knowledge within the home.

For a number of reasons, the foundations needed for the home of clients who may have experienced a chaotic or changeable lifestyle will probably be difficult to identify. There will be many aspects to life that will need to be clarified; through my book you can help with enabling individuals to discover and unravel what these might be.

The chances are high that anybody living a chaotic lifestyle in a home where there are no feelings of attachment, will create a chaotic lifestyle outside the home too. By being involved and directing the way the home is created, your clients will very tentatively begin to develop some attachment, thereby breaking this cycle.

To help the people you work with succeed in creating the very best home for themselves, you will need to work towards instilling trust between you. Individuals will need to feel they can be honest about their feelings and that you are a person to talk to and share ideas with. Only with this type of trust can your clients begin to rely on and take seriously their own inner thoughts, allowing for understanding on a deeper level of what they need and want out of life as well as what is truly valued.

1.2 Exploring Values

Although my book can be worked through in any order, once this Concept is covered, the sections that follow will be made easier but, as always, you must be guided by your clients.

Before anybody can begin to think about what their needs are with regard to creating foundations for a home, they will need to try to have some understanding about their own value system. You can help individuals to gain this knowledge and then to apply it to creating a home and living their lives.

Our values are an integral part of who we are. They can

influence our behaviour and our character. They are qualities of our inner selves and although it is possible to go through life not acknowledging them, they are still there, and are very much about us as individuals.

The list below provides a few common values that a lot of people share; ask your clients to think of a few of their own too and then use their ideas to open up a discussion, just see where the conversation goes.

Honesty

Respect

Peace

Success

Security

Bravery

Love

Decisiveness

Dependability

Drive

The values we hold can directly affect the way we live. For example, they may determine how we spend our leisure time, what work we want to do, what our religious beliefs or our politics are. We are able to deliberately change some of our values and some will change naturally according to our circumstances or our life experiences. Others will remain immoveable and will be with us throughout our entire lives – these are our core values.

By identifying core values, you will be providing your clients with a valuable tool to use in many areas of life. Identifying them though, is only the start of the process. Core values will be of no use if, once understood, they are not used to their full advantage. Because the foundations to an individual's home will be an integral part of who he or she is, when understood, core values can be integrated into these foundations, ultimately underpinning their life and creating the holding place for past experiences.

Unfortunately some people never know and never seem to want to know what their core values are. These people often lead their lives feeling frustrated or unfulfilled, feeling that there might be something missing but not quite knowing what it is or how to identify it. You can help your clients to avoid living this way.

Our core values should not be confused with our goals in life, these are something different. However, if we set goals that are in harmony with our values, then we are more likely to achieve them.

The list below shows some of the areas core values can originate from, use these for discussions in your work to enable individuals to understand where their own personal influences are coming from.

Parents or carers

Religious institutions

Employers

Neighbours, friends

Peers

Teachers

Media

Places of study

Politicians

Clubs

Some are inherited

Your clients may have adopted all sorts of values from a variety of sources, and may still be at the stage where they are unfixed. During this time individuals can find themselves swinging backwards and forwards with ideas and opinions as they consider their own feelings and thoughts alongside those of people around them.

There may be some inner conflict too, and although it is always important to respect the values of other people, it should not be at the expense of our own. Living out other people's values doesn't work well for any of us, we end up not being true to ourselves. As your clients try to identify what is really important, you will need to allow the time and space for this to happen, only this way will values which are still being worked out, gradually come to the fore.

Below are a few suggestions of why different people might want to instil their own values in somebody else. You can use these in your discussions or to illustrate a point where appropriate.

- Employers – they will want to maximise the work performance and therefore profit.

- Media – when people identify with the values they represent, they will sell more papers, magazines, television and radio will be more popular.

- Peers – to gain power, to dominate or control.

- Family – parents might want their children to adopt the same values as themselves so that things continue along the same route, thus avoiding change. Siblings may also want to gain control over each other.

- Politicians – to gain power or control.

It isn't always as black and white as this but these examples show how vulnerable we all are to the pressures around us every day. Working out personal core values will help your clients feel confident about creating a framework by which to live.

Below is a list of some of the possible benefits gained once a value system is in place and then implemented in creating a home. Ask your clients to provide a few reasons for themselves and then use the list to help with promoting more ideas for discussion.

- Values can keep us on track for the way we live, we can refer to these when we feel confused about what to do.

- They can provide a path in life and help develop direction, this can be with work, study or with an interest or hobby. They can also help to open up opportunities for interests.

- We have a clearer understanding of some fundamental issues in life such as world conflict or persecution.

- With a value system there is less inner conflict, we have real understanding of who we are.

- Time is not wasted on things that don't sit comfortably with our values.

- Our values can be referred to when important decisions need to be made.

- We can make the right choices for ourselves about people we get involved with, places we visit or projects we support.

All of these benefits are 'best case' scenarios but without core values it is likely that your clients will feel out of control or unconnected to their inner lives. This can lead to internal conflict and confusion, with the individual having no hint about where these feelings might be coming from.

There are many simple ways of identifying personal core values. Below are some basic questions that you can use, each of them may hold more than one answer.

What do you feel passionate about?

What did you enjoy doing when you were a child?

When you are at your happiest, what are you doing?

The answers to these questions will provide a general idea of what drives an individual and what they feel is important. These are genuine inner feelings and need to be taken seriously. As you continue to work on this subject, you will find that the ideas and answers developing will become clearer and more precise.

Be Specific

When your clients are used to the idea of developing values, then they can work towards defining them, writing down around ten things that are important right now is a good starting point.

This list can consist of things that bring out passion as well as attitudes. Individuals may need to be given some ideas about how to decide what is important, a good way to break through with this is to identify a person they admire. You can then encourage them to think about why they admire them, what has this person achieved, what is attractive about them or the way they live. Why would somebody want to be like them? These answers could provide important things to put on the list. If only one or two things come up then work with these. If a person really struggles and no ideas arise, then use the list below.

Simplicity

Positive attitude

Playing sport

Inner peace

Money

Privacy

Trust

Dancing

Honesty

Having a house

You can see that some of the things on this list are actual values and some are not, some values need to be identified. For example, cycling might be on the list; whilst this is not a value in itself, the values within it could be 'achievement, challenge or self-discipline'. Within managing money, which could also be on the list, the values might be 'self-respect or discipline'.

During your work you may find that your clients hold conflicting values. Whilst popularity might be something to be desired, so might privacy. Only the individual can work out which one will take priority and, to an extent, the one which is left will be put aside.

When a list has been settled on, you can help to put the values in order of importance. Any repeats can be crossed out, likewise with the least important ones. This will need to be done several times until the list is refined down to around five. These will be the core values.

Values in the Home

There are many ways to bring core values into a home. For example, if only Fair Trade products are used the values of respect and fairness are implemented.

The list below shows how a selection of core values can be brought into your clients' daily lives within a home.

Respect	**Look after accommodation, respect own needs**
Fairness	**Pay rent on time**
	Use products that have not been tested on animals
Caring	**Invite a friend round for company or a meal**
	Offer to help somebody
	Have a treat sometimes
Challenge	**Live independently, stretch own capabilities**
	Play sport
Friends	**Maintain boundaries**
	Be honest and reliable

The important thing about using personally worked-out values to create the foundations for a home is that views and opinions are being outwardly demonstrated and seen every day. This then validates and reinforces what can at times be a very fragile identity. Gradually a stronger sense of self will develop and enhance the ability to expand thinking to beyond the everyday and out into the wider world.

Arriving at core values can be a protracted process, but if you are patient and sensitive in your work, you will enable individuals to learn how to express themselves through their homes. I am not suggesting for a minute that anybody will sail through this without some real work on your part and you may well meet with some resistance. However, you will be opening up opportunities for individuals to acquire some real knowledge and understanding about themselves, standing them in good stead for creating something permanent and personal within their lives. Very slowly, the importance of home will increase for them and a new perspective of what it can provide will emerge.

Living at Home

To help you continue to challenge what might be limiting views of home held by your clients, the questions below can be used to initiate thoughts, ideas and discussions.

- Ask your client how it feels to have a day off, completely free from any commitments or arrangements. Is this seen as an opportunity to relax at home or is there a need to get out at the earliest opportunity? If it is the latter, try to discuss why this is.

- Ask if the home is used for doing things that bring pleasure, or are all the nice things saved for outside the home? If they are, try to talk about what makes it like this.

- Find out if the home is used as a place for reflection or valuable quiet time at all. If it is not, encourage your clients to talk about why.

There will always be valid reasons why clients feel it's too difficult to make an emotional investment into a home they feel no connection with; spending time somewhere else therefore becomes an attractive and easier option for them. It is quite likely that the majority of the people you work with will run and organise their lives away from their accommodation. Through your work you will enable them to gradually gain some insight into just what a home can provide, this will lead them to the understanding that it can be so much more than just somewhere to eat and sleep. They will start to be open to the idea that a home can be an integral part of who they are and that it has the power to provide them with dependable security. This factor alone can strongly affect how they feel on a daily basis and consequently how they go about their daily lives.

1.3 All About Passion

Projects:

Ideas Poster

List of New Things to Try

Picture of Long-Term Goal

Foundations to a home need to be built around the whole of who an individual is. This means that the future is as important as the past or the present.

When you take your clients through this section of the book you will need to instil optimism as well as hope and belief in their ambitions for the future. It is important for individuals to understand that their dreams provide a strong thread running through their being and that this thread will be one of the building blocks that will form the foundations you are trying to help establish.

There are no limits to the number of ambitions anybody can have but before they can be used constructively towards creating a home, they need to be clearly identified. Some of us are fortunate enough to know immediately what inspires or excites us but some of us may not know this straight away.

Firstly there needs to be a belief that anything is possible; as long as there is a passion for it, then effort can be made to achieve it. An important part of the experience of having a dream is not necessarily the sense of achievement on realising that dream, it is more about the journey we go through as we get closer to reaching our goal.

A lot of ambitions are never actually realised, or certainly not for a very long time. This doesn't mean that during the time spent working towards them things are not being achieved. If your clients have clear achievable goals to believe in they will work better generally, motivation will improve and self-esteem will grow.

You will need considerable skill and patience but you can begin to tune in to what individuals feel strongly about by being aware of their interests. The list below provides you with some ideas about what might appeal to them and you can look out for any real attraction shown. However, there may be many others that you will soon begin to notice and pick up on.

Animals or the outdoors

Music, listening to or creating

Sport, taking part as well as watching

Favourite television or radio programmes

Books

Heroes

Conversations with friends, what makes it exciting

Listen carefully during your conversations to what is really being said

If you start to pay close attention to your clients' interests you will gradually get to know where their hearts are. Talk to them, find out what excites them, you might be surprised at what they really feel about something, and how far they might like to go with it.

Below are some questions that will help you to initiate discussions. Remember, passion is driven by individual and personal desires so, encourage individuals to listen to their hearts. The main point of the exercise is to recognise and listen to what is central to who they are; this part of their true nature is really important and sometimes a little prompting is all it takes to get in touch with it.

- Think about the things you have achieved at different stages of your life. How do they make you feel now? Why do they make you feel this way? Would you want to take them further now?

- Do you like to be different from others but are held back because you feel embarrassed or worried about what people might think? Forget everyone else, focus on yourself, and think about what you would like to be brave enough to do

- What do you think other people like about you? Is this the real you or are you trying to please?

- If you didn't have to worry about failure, what would you do, why would you do it and how would you feel?

- If you didn't have to earn money, how would you spend your days?

- Who do you admire and why? These are the people you are using as potential role models, think about why this is.

It is so easy for these thoughts and feelings to get buried under all sorts of other issues in a client's life and the time and effort you put in to help tease them out is invaluable. The result will be a gradual and real understanding of how it feels to be in tune with and led by the higher self. This will have a positive effect on your clients and in the list below are just some of the things they might begin to experience when this happens.

Feelings of freedom

Feeling rejuvenated

Motivation

Feeling that nothing is impossible

Knowing this is their real self

Better coping abilities

Fewer worries

Sadly, it is so easy for the people you work with to lose sight of this in themselves but you can begin to show how to put this session of work into place within a home and make the results an integral part of a new life.

Project:

Ideas Poster

The main idea behind this project is that it will get your clients' imaginations flowing – they will begin to think about things they really want to do. Once they begin to have ideas, others will follow, these can be written down and displayed within a home and nothing needs to be set in stone, ideas can evolve and change. The time spent on this project will provide valuable opportunities for thinking and talking which you can use to introduce other aspects of the book.

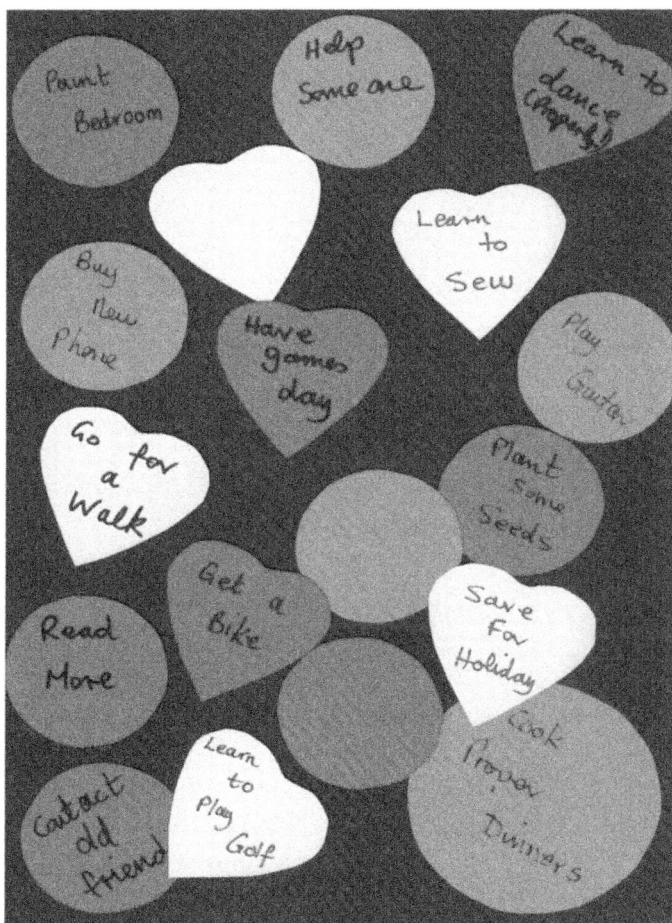

For the project you will need some coloured card, cut to around A4 size or larger if your client has lots of ideas. Some smaller brightly coloured card or paper cut to heart, star or circular shapes, the brighter the colours the better. Some reusable adhesive and two or three coloured marker pens.

Spend some time brainstorming ideas for a list of things to do or try. Write one idea on one of the small shapes, continue with this until all the ideas are written on the shapes. Use a small piece of adhesive to arrange and stick these onto the larger piece of card then display it somewhere prominent.

This same idea can be used to remind your clients of things they are interested in and want to look up and read about.

Project:

List of New Things to Try

This project takes the ideas poster a little further as it narrows down and focuses on fewer options. These need to be the ones your clients can feel serious about and are prepared to put some effort into achieving. Again, you will need a piece of coloured card, a few small shaped pieces and some marker pens. You will also need a straight edge to rule some lines.

Firstly, draw a line down the centre of the card and on one side write the heading, 'New Things I Want To Try', on the other write, 'What It Was Like'. Write down ideas they can work towards doing on the smaller shaped coloured card and stick them under the first heading. Keep these simple and achievable so just three or four is enough. By each shape, rule up two or three lines for writing down thoughts and feelings after trying something new. For example, would they do it again, how often, and if not, why not? Your clients can then display this where it can easily be seen, it will inspire them to actually go out and do different things and create a sense of achievement with the reflections.

Project:

Long-Term Goal

Again, this project is a simple way to keep your clients' long term goals alive. Their goals might be anything from owning a house to going on a special holiday or having a career of their choice.

Although the images illustrated are basic, they incorporate a lot. In order to achieve something like this your clients will need to be disciplined, fit, reliable and have vision. To create the project you will need card, around A4 size, and an image of the dream along with a picture of the client you are working with. If the dream happens to be owning a car, a picture of the vehicle can be used with the photograph of the client sitting in it or standing by it. Whatever the image is, use adhesive to stick it on the card. The whole thing can then be decorated in their own style and put somewhere prominent. Remember though that as your clients change and grow, so probably will the long-term goals.

Those Lightbulb Moments

Generally speaking, the seed for a passion or a dream is sparked by a particular event or experience; you can help your clients to recognise when their imagination was fired and what inspired their dreams. When they identify the moment that this happened, you can talk about why it was so significant, this will help with understanding what is important, what they would love to achieve and why.

I know somebody whose ambition was inspired by the film 'The Graduate', it gave him the drive to save up for a very long time in order to buy a sports car. Because of this inspiration he became motivated to commit to work, save money, stick to a plan and achieve his goal. Within the context of my book, this person should have a picture of Mrs Robinson in his home to remind him how his determination and hard work paid off.

Representing these moments, and clearly there can be more than one, in the home will send a powerful self-affirming message to your clients. It doesn't matter whether the dream has been achieved, or at what stage it is, the important thing is to keep it alive and let it speak about the individual.

As an example, when I was a child I was inspired by the summers I spent with relatives in Wales. Ever since this time my dream has been to run a smallholding in Wales. There are a number of ways I bring my dream into my home and these have evolved and changed over the years. This doesn't matter, there are no rules and whatever feels right for your clients is right.

This picture epitomises the experiences that inspired me, my aunty lived what is now part of my dream. Realistically, I know that her life was frugal and hard and I don't think I want to recreate that, but she gave me my ambition and enabled me to see something different.

My dream still influences me, where I go for time out, my hobbies and interests and where I choose to live. More importantly though, even today it underpins who I am, and the small steps along the way, like keeping a few ducks, enabled me to feel closer to my ideal. It doesn't matter that I don't live on a smallholding in Wales, it's the value of the dream that is so important and, because it has been with me for such a long time, it really is part of my character.

The picture was taken completely by chance, it represents all of this to me and hangs in my kitchen where I see it every day. Not only do I feel a sense of security when I see the photograph of my aunty, which is the same feeling I had on her smallholding as a child, but I am inwardly encouraged and strengthened to continue to believe in who I really am.

Dreams and passions are as different as the individuals who have them. They need to be taken seriously because they are representative of who we are and can underpin our identity. With your help your clients' inner lives of dreams and ideals can be explored and used as a tool to create firm foundations on which to build a home and a life. Gradually they really will become more and more aware of the connection between themselves and their accommodation.

Do you think your clients already have any special mementos in their possession that could represent a dream? As we have discussed before, the individuals you work with will need to trust you before they will be able to share this intimate information. Show them you are genuine, use the list below to help you do this.

Discuss subjects a client shows an interest in

Actively listen

Help with research

Encourage small steps along the way

Show kindness

Help with making plans

Help to keep a focus

An individual's ambitions can be used in many ways to enhance a home. The ideas below will help to get you started and your clients may come up with more; encourage them to let go of their inhibitions, there are no rules!

- Pictures, photos or promotional information of whatever the dream might be.

- Something to represent the original spark of inspiration such as a picture of Mrs Robinson.

- Souvenirs of steps along the way. When I had my ducks I kept a blown and decorated duck egg, it represented so much more to me than a duck!

- Something tangible to represent the very personal journey of trying to achieve a goal which might seem a long way off. When I was teaching yoga I always kept a piece of Indian fabric in my bedroom, this reminded me that one day I would see where it all started.

- Display a significant item of clothing such as a woolly hat to represent a sponsored walk or a trip up Snowdon.

- Find a spot to show a relevant piece of equipment for activity, for example a climbing hook or canoe paddle, depending of course on the interest.

- Personal affirmations, help your clients to design their own and place them where they can be seen every day.

Project:

Create Personal Affirmations

Designs for affirmations should be fun. They need to be eye catching with a simple and positive message. Work with your clients to experiment with ideas and establish what they want to say; it doesn't have to stop at one, the more positive messages people see about themselves the better. Then, the affirmations can be written on small pieces of card or coloured paper which can be propped up or fixed where they can be seen every day. On a mirror is good or over a worktop or sink. Don't forget the artwork, encourage individuals to decorate them in their own style.

To help get you started, use the ideas below.

I believe in myself

I am free to think my own thoughts

I express my feelings

I can make new friends

I will dance

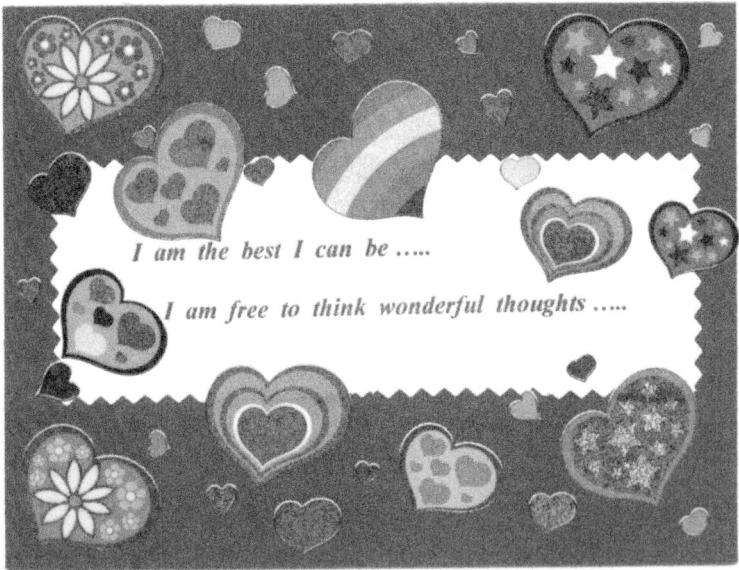

Displaying personal affirmations is a powerful thing to do, they not only show an individual's personality but will help to keep a vision in sight. They are a useful tool too for clients to use to speak about themselves to others.

For an individual to achieve success they have to believe it is possible. Having constant reminders around the home boosting self-esteem will encourage this belief as well as develop respect for their own individuality.

Can it Happen?

Unfortunately, even though your clients may identify their ambitions, self-doubt can soon begin to creep in, leading them to question what they can actually achieve. A good way through this is for individuals to spend some time considering what type of person they are. For example, are they somebody to take what they want seriously, believing that making plans and staying focussed will provide a good chance of success, or, are they somebody who lives in the belief that one day, magically, it will all just happen?

Sadly, the latter is more likely to be the answer so you will need to encourage your clients to consider realistically, how they can go about achieving what they want.

Below are some of the ways you can help with this.

- Make plans – these need to be short, mid and long-term.

- Set achievable goals that take into account time, money, levels of fitness.

- Look at the time needed to work towards the end goal, be realistic.

- Take into account the time needed to work and live, remember that ordinary life goes on.

- Finance – where will this come from?

- Equipment – where to get it, how to use it.

- Education – what needs to be learnt?

- One step at a time, it should be a pleasure!

Make sure your clients are reminded that it doesn't matter what the goal is, if it comes from the heart, it will be central to their character. Being able to explore ideas around this subject with the possibility of displaying them within the home provides a wonderful feeling of being grounded, of somehow knowing that all is possible.

Just Believe

Sustaining belief in an ambition over a long period of time can be incredibly hard for clients who lack fundamental belief in themselves or who have a fragile sense of self.

When this is the case they might inadvertently put their lives in the hands of people who don't have their best interests at heart. Mixing with people who believe in failure rather than success can be very detrimental to the individuals you work with because, with this influence, they will believe in it too. There will be various reasons why clients will want these people in their lives, they might not want to be seen as an outsider, not want to upset people, they may also be in close relationships with some of them. It is therefore easier to lose sight of what they really want and comply with the negative thinkers. It is possible that, despite nurturing a secret ambition for years, individuals will listen to these influences to such an extent that they will eventually let their dream go.

While using my book it will be your role to counterbalance any pessimistic influences in your clients' lives and challenge any negative perceptions they have of themselves. If your clients continue to believe that the negative thinkers know best, then it will be almost impossible for them to realistically achieve what they really want.

Influences of this nature can come from many different sources and for a variety of complicated reasons. The list below is a selection of possibilities. Use it to raise awareness in your clients and also with yourself, then use it as an aid to enable individuals to gain understanding of some of their own approaches to life.

Birth parents

Siblings

Friends, peers

Extended family

Work, school, college

Negativity is something we all have to deal with but you can show your clients that we all have the same fears and feelings of inadequacy. Let them know that you are no different, and let them see that despite this, you continue to believe in yourself in order to achieve the life you want.

Knowing you have somebody who believes in you can change your life. Many years ago when the yoga class I was attending was going to lose its teacher, it was suggested I might like to take the group over. I didn't have nearly enough belief in myself to think this would be possible, and certainly couldn't do anything about it.

A few weeks later and after several discussions, as I started to try to think about why I had been invited to do this, my perception of who I was began to change. With the knowledge that several people believed I could do it I began to think that maybe I was capable enough and that I really could take some training. Taking the class started to become a reality for me and my confidence gradually grew. This happened simply because, despite still having some negative influences around me, I chose to believe the positive thinkers and began to allow myself to believe it could work. Once I had agreed, a whole new world opened up to me.

The point is, nothing had changed, I hadn't done any training, I knew no more than I previously knew. The only thing that had happened is that I had been shown that people believed in me, in my ability to take on something I thought I had no chance of achieving. I decided to trust them on their judgement and my life changed. I went on to become a qualified yoga teacher and taught for more than twenty years.

Although the work you are doing with your clients will be in very small steps and may at times seem slow, the importance of it must never be underestimated. You have the opportunity to empower individuals, enabling them to believe they really can do it, whatever it is.

If individuals are going to be successful in independence, they will almost certainly need to reduce the impact of negative influences within their lives. Your gentle work with them in this area will heighten awareness of what is going on around them and gradually, they will feel able to make this happen.

1.4 Potential Obstacles

Anything introduced into anybody's life that represent change can be unsettling. Because your work with my book involves identifying and laying down the foundations for a home and a future life, it will almost certainly be seen by most of your clients as, at the least unnerving, and at the worst, frightening and challenging. As you work through some of the issues raised they may experience a mixture of feelings and at times it might feel a bit like an emotional roller coaster, both for them and for you.

To prepare you both for what might be to come, some of the more common feelings associated with change are below, happily you will see that not all of them are negatives!

Feeling stretched

Fear

Doubt

Anxiety

Feeling unsettled

Brief periods of feeling strong

Feel more imaginative

See things in new light

All of these things need to be taken into consideration and your work will need to be sensitive, but your clients, whatever age they are, are learning how to use their personalities and experiences as tools to live in a new way. This will break with old habits and ways of thinking, both within the home and outside it. Gradually as your work goes on individuals will begin to see the very clear link between the quality of home and the quality of life.

However well-intentioned everybody is, whenever there is change happening, there will be obstacles along the way. You can help your clients to be prepared and therefore more likely to succeed by bringing some of these to the fore.

The more common problems occurring are below, encourage open discussion about the real possibilities of some of them happening.

Running out of money

No time

No energy

Change of timetable or venue

Health problems

Despondency and disappointment

Solutions to these problems are shown below, discuss all the options including other ideas that your clients will come up with.

Find some sort of work, cut down on spending
Reorganise timetable, prioritise workload
Regulate sleep pattern and diet
Rethink travel or reschedule things
Take some time out, slow down, get fit, it's not a race
Be realistic, set achievable goals

Achieving your ambition doesn't happen overnight, there will always be obstacles arising but the whole point of having them is that they provide hope and something to strive towards. This in itself will help to keep potential problems at bay and in turn provide energy and enthusiasm as well as a real sense of purpose.

While I was training for my yoga diploma my home was full of everything to do with yoga. Pictures of postures I wanted to learn about, books I wanted to read; I researched out yogic diet so items in my kitchen changed and I even changed the way I dressed. Anybody coming into my home at that time would have seen my dream. I created an environment for myself that absolutely affirmed who I was and what I wanted to achieve. Your clients can do the same.

They are the only ones to know how much they want to reveal about themselves to others but when they are able to display things openly and comfortably in their own living environment it will boost self-confidence and gradually develop a stronger sense of pride and self-worth.

You can help individuals realise that although there is a starting and an ending point in reaching goals it is actually the bit in between that is so important. Striving towards goals can take many years but the journey, and the many stages they will pass through during this time will be their lives, and this is what will contribute so greatly towards building character.

During this time, everything your clients get involved with, the people they meet, their achievements, places they visit, will ultimately all become an integral part of their history. Goals should always be displayed prominently in the home, but so should evidence of all the work and effort being made every day as they travel towards them.

Steps along the way will help anybody prepare for potential problems. The list below is an example for someone who wants to learn how to canoe, however you can apply this to learning any new skill.

Find out how and where it can be learnt

Improve level of fitness

Learn to swim

Work out expenditure, cost of lessons, travel, equipment

Books, read as much as possible on the subject

Spend time talking to others who already do it

Watch people doing it

Find out what equipment and clothing is necessary

Logistics, time needed to travel and practice

How to raise funds

Even though it might take a long time to achieve, as individuals work towards their goals there will be significant impact along the way and the rewards are enormous. When people start to realise they can do it, they experience feelings of excitement, exhilaration, confidence and soaring self-esteem.

By believing in and striving towards long-term aims your clients will inadvertently begin to provide for themselves the very thing they most need – strong and long-lasting foundations which will be the beginnings of a stable and secure home and life.

1.5 Mission Statements Matter

Project:

Personal Mission Statement

With the development of core values and by identifying passions and ambitions your clients will be in a position to create a Personal Mission Statement to help them stay focused.

A Mission Statement is a very individual thing, there are

no right or wrong ways to create one and nothing will be set in stone. Your clients' statements will reflect who they are and what their lives are about at the time they are created. When completed, it can be displayed within the home and used as a powerful personal message.

Writing a Statement might take a while, some individuals may need to draft and redraft to get the words right and sometimes it's a good idea to put it away for a while and then go back to it with fresh eyes. Even after it's finished, as life changes, the Statement may well be revised again.

To help your clients get started with this project you can show some examples of what a Mission Statement is all about.

Below are some simple ideas that can be handwritten or produced on a computer and then decorated in any way your clients choose. There are many choices about what to write them on, from coloured card to simple printer paper. The important thing is that it reflects the ideas and personality of the person creating it and what they see as their purpose in life.

It is always my intention to…

Have Fun

Be a Good Friend

Manage Money

Believe in Myself

I Believe I Can…

Look After Myself

Show Respect

Finish Everything I Start

Stay Out of Debt

To Have the Life I Want I Will...

Achieve my goals. Respect my home and manage money in a way that keeps me out of debt. I will remember how much friends mean to me.

Once your clients have created their Statement then you can help them to decide on a way of displaying it within the home.

The list below will provide you with some suggestions but your clients may well come up with something of their own, go with their ideas.

Print from a computer using different colours or fonts

Handwrite it out with decorative script

Decorate it with pictures or symbols your clients can relate to, either cut out or hand drawn

Mount and frame it

Use a clip frame

Laminate it

Prop it up or hang it on a wall

A Safe Haven Within the Context of Home

We all need an anchor and a sanctuary where we can feel safe from the world when life becomes unavoidably difficult, and the individuals you are supporting may well need it more than most. What makes a place safe for one person may not be the same for others, what your clients will need in order to feel safe will depend upon past experiences, good and not so good, their interests, as well as hopes and ambitions. By reflecting on these things they will gain some insight into what they really need to feel safe and why.

Below is a selection of meanings for a safe haven, use this to promote discussion with your clients, they may identify with some of them and may well be able to add more.

Place to think

Place to heal

Somewhere quiet

Place for rest

No time limits

No pressures

No threats

It would be good to prompt thoughts around how the home has been used in the past. For example, has it been a place of safety? Was this a place to get away from it all? If this was not the case, make some gentle enquiries about why. If the home is to be a stabilising influence on life, it is crucial that it feels safe and secure.

Very often, what we want from our homes and what we actually get are two very different things. We might look on our homes as places of sanctuary and yet deep down inside we know something is missing. Unfortunately we often can't quite work out what this is. For most of us we haven't got the time or energy to think too much about it and we get by. For your clients it is crucial that you help them identify just what it will take for a home to become a sanctuary.

A safe home will evoke all sorts of positive emotions, below is a selection of what anybody could expect to feel.

Safe

Peaceful

Organised

Free of demands

Comfortable

Secure

Calm

Warm

If your clients' homes are to influence their lives they will need to feel most of these things, however, this might be difficult for them to recognise to begin with. The projects within my book provide you with opportunities to build trust and openness between you, but you will need to be prepared to take time and patience while an individual begins the slow and gradual process of looking upon a home in a different way.

The Haven in 'Safe Haven'

Project:

Memory Box

One of the key features of a safe home is a feeling of calm. One of the first things to look at in order to create a calm environment is ways of reducing mayhem or chaos within the space. This means getting organised. Organisation is the crux of calmness and you can start your work on this with your clients by helping them to separate out some of the different aspects of organisation.

Below are the basics for getting things under control.

Declutter

Create a place for everything

Create transitional areas

Make lists

Get into routines

If your clients' homes are going to feel like a haven they need to be able to walk through the door and not feel overwhelmed with things waiting to be done. Their understanding will be that, although the world is sometimes a chaotic place, a home doesn't have to be.

This part of the book can be exciting and rewarding but not without its challenges as your clients will have to face a little reality around what their accommodation might actually consist of.

Decluttering

The first basic step then, is to thin things down a little. Everybody's home is a precious space, and should not be full of items that are not useful or good to look at. If your clients have things in their possession they haven't used for a year, then they probably don't need them. They will find it hard at first, thinking that there might come a day when something will come in handy, but you can encourage them to be ruthless and unemotional; space will be at a premium and they will be amazed at how liberating it is to actually clear space and life of unnecessary clutter.

Decluttering, however, can be an emotive thing, and the impact shouldn't be underestimated. To an outsider, the amount of clutter a client owns might look unnecessary, but every item will have a story behind it and a good reason to be kept. It is here that your skills and your relationship with your clients will play a significant part. This is training for their future so it will be crucial for you to lead individuals to the understanding that it is alright to let go of some items. Everything that needs to be kept can be put into order and appropriate storage.

This first step towards getting organised will have a dramatic effect on the way an individual feels, not only about personal space, which will appear calmer and more spacious, but also about creating some understanding within themselves.

Sorting belongings in this way provides your clients with opportunities to reclaim personal history. Gradually as things are put into physical order, memories and experiences will slowly become much clearer and will begin to feel less random on their recollection. Knowing that the items a client wants to hold on to are safely organised will bring about feelings of being in control, of things being stable, not only of the past but also of life today.

There are numerous reasons why people don't declutter. Some of them are listed below but remember, the work you are doing with your clients is not just a glorified tidying up session, it is part of the process of setting down the basics for an organised and safe home, so stick with it, encourage and support all the way.

I need everything I have

I can't part with things other people have bought me

I have got clothes I haven't worn but I might need them

I might need it if I take up a hobby

I don't want to throw something away and then find I need it

Some of these may well change into:

I cleared the lot and felt great

Apart from the last answer, any reasons such as these are a block to creating a calm environment. Your clients may have very different and complex reasons for not thinning things down but, if you really want to help them achieve what they need, you will have to stay focused on your work.

To get started you will need to provide plenty of black sacks or cardboard boxes. Clean and undamaged items can go to charity shops or a boot sale, the rest can be recycled or taken to the skip.

Decluttering sounds a simple idea, however, it can be a very complex issue and an emotional minefield so you will need lots of patience. Somehow, we all tend to think that we feel safer when we accumulate lots of possessions and that security comes by never changing things. Sadly, this is a complete myth because the time we really begin to feel safe is when we have gained control over our environment by freeing ourselves from unnecessary possessions and clutter. By simplifying and thinning things down, your clients will do just this and will not only find they have a calmer environment, they will also have cleared their minds.

Once the declutter has been done it is time to introduce the 'one in, one out' rule. This is the rule that means if your clients buy something new, something old needs to be gotten rid of, whatever this might be. This may seem like a tough principal to live by but, by implementing it they will be encouraged to think twice before buying anything, thus easing the strain on finances and important living space.

Clearly, there will be sentimental items that your clients will need to keep. For these you can show them how to create a memory box. This is a powerful exercise in tidying up experiences and memories and an excellent way to keep important and significant mementos. Designing and creating this and then using it in the home will bring about a sense of order and permanence.

For this project your clients will need a suitable box – a strong shoe box is ideal. Cut out enough small images to cover the box, these can be of anything individuals like including photographs. The cutting doesn't have to be precise because the shapes will overlap each other. You will need craft glue and some clear varnish. Put the lid on the box and draw a line around the box where the lid ends. Avoid sticking anything above this line or the lid won't fit back on. Just take one image at a time and stick it on the box until the whole box and lid is covered. When the glue is dry, usually a few hours, give a thin coat of PVA mixed with water to seal. Then put a coat of varnish over when this is dry.

Your clients might like to create more than one of these, a good way to keep organised is to have one for every year or to use a larger one for special memory joggers of particular times or people.

By working on this project individuals will be able to recognise significant and meaningful times in their lives and be able to 'put them away' in safety. This works on a practical level and an emotional level. With your support clients will be able to spend time sorting through their history and learn to take time to really value how they feel about it, this will significantly reduce the chances of their pasts jeopardising their futures.

1.6 A Place for Everything

By introducing some simple ideas around tidiness you can help your clients to create a home environment that will aid and not hinder them.

The simplest way to tidiness is to have a place for everything. Below are some basic but efficient ideas for keeping a space looking orderly.

Hanging space: If there is a shortage of this in your clients' accommodation then a few extra hooks can be put on to the backs of doors. Put one or two on the entrance doors for coats and bags, and in the bedroom they are brilliant for hanging clothes on hangers. In the bathroom besides towels, toilet or cosmetic bags can also be hung up as well as a laundry bag for washing. Hooks are cheap, simple and effective. They enable you to feel you have put things away, as well as keeping things off the floor or furniture. For clients they are a simple way to get into good habits around tidiness; they won't have to open a door or fold anything, just hang it up.

Shoe tidy: Shoes can be enemies of tidiness and need a designated space, preferably by the entrance door. This doesn't need to be anything fancy, a shoe rack or shelf is good but the floor will work too. It really is just a matter of getting into the habit of putting shoes in the same place when arriving home.

Keys/Phone: There will need to be a container of some kind by the entrance door for a mobile phone and keys. This is an opportunity for your clients to use something personal, maybe a souvenir mug or dish of some kind, maybe a box that something special arrived in, as long as it means something, it will be good to use. This presents a good opportunity for you to discuss the item chosen, why is it significant. What memories does it hold? What feelings does it evoke? To see and use it every day will affirm all of this and promote feelings of well-being on going out and coming home.

Paper and post: Junk mail and papers can all be an issue for anybody trying to keep things tidy. You will need to try to encourage your clients to get into the habit of binning the rubbish straight away. They will need to have a designated place for anything that is important or needs attention and also get into the habit of dealing with it regularly. It would be a good idea to encourage sorting any paperwork at least once a week on the same day or evening so that it becomes second nature.

Toiletries/cosmetics: These items really need to be kept together and in an ideal world this would be in a bathroom but, it is possible that your clients may be sharing this space so personal belongings left here might not be safe. It doesn't really matter where they are kept, the point is to allocate a place for them, and to experience and understand how it feels not to have things lying around everywhere.

It is quite likely that individuals you support will have got used to the feelings of confusion and anxiety which often surrounds a disorderly way of life. Learning how to create a calm and ordered lifestyle and being confident about maintaining it will go a long way to breaking the cycle of disorderly living.

Tidiness is something that needs to be worked on, there will be many times in your clients' lives when they will not want to worry about it. The last thing they will want to feel is pressure so, for these inevitable times there needs to be a plan.

Transitional Areas: You can show how to create a couple of temporary areas for anything and everything to be put until an individual has more time and energy or just feels more motivated. To do this you will need two containers, maybe baskets or plastic boxes, big enough to take a couple of items of clothing, some books and DVDs. Place one in the bedroom and another by the entrance door; these areas should only be used as a last resort but as the routine of using them becomes second nature, they will be the first place to look when items go missing.

Being able to find things when they are needed is incredibly important to show your clients what being in control feels like. Simple things like this will help to avoid those awful feelings of frustration, confusion and sometimes panic which can arise on a daily basis.

Put it on the list

Lists are another basic but incredibly important tool your clients can use to create organisation in the home. Lists are a way of dealing with the clutter that you can feel but you can't see.

If any of us wants to be in control of our homes and our lives then we need to get things out of our heads and onto paper. Lists are an essential part of staying on top of things and if this is going to be a new routine for your clients then one list a day is a good start. You will need to encourage them not to be over ambitious, it needs to be achievable, if it is unrealistic they won't complete all the tasks and will feel a failure.

Nothing is too small to go on a list, if it needs doing then it needs to be written down. It can be very satisfying too, to cross things off when they're done.

Once your clients get into the habit of working with a daily list they can start to make a weekly one and gradually move on to a monthly one. These longer-term ones can set deadlines for more ambitious tasks like finishing a project or painting a room.

When introducing this practice, a good place to start is with the continuous shopping list; as soon as they start running low on something it needs to go on the list. The impact of helping individuals to become familiar with a routine this simple before moving to independence cannot be overstated, it will avoid all sorts of frustrations and confusions in the home.

Around the shopping list will be a whole range of other tasks to tackle, like setting time aside regularly to plan meals for the coming week and putting them on the meals list. To help with shopping clients will need to check what is in the fridge and cupboard, try to encourage them to be adventurous and to avoid the habit of having the same meal on the same day of the week.

Good simple routines will underpin your clients' success in their new accommodation. If they can get used to them before moving then they will be second nature when the move happens.

1.7 Routine and Structure

Simple routine and structure can add immense value to your clients' everyday lives. To begin with, routines can appear boring and predictably dull. You are in a position to enable individuals to see things differently. Usually, the people who use routine to underpin their daily lives are far from boring, these are the motivated, organised people who get all their mundane chores done speedily, leaving plenty of free time to do the things they really want to do.

With routine comes an amount of predictability about life and this in turn will bring about feelings of security, of being safe and of being in control. If your clients feel in control within their homes, they will soon begin to feel it in their lives. You can introduce practical ideas around basic routine and structure, therefore laying down the start of what should become habits of a lifetime. Your clients can begin to carry out some of the suggestions and, as the benefits of living this way begin to be understood and felt, self-esteem and confidence will grow. Individuals will find they have the confidence and energy to enjoy the potential of using their spare time doing things they enjoy.

To establish routines that will stand any chance of survival your clients will need to take into account any existing commitments, training or work for example, plus any other obligations. It would be a good idea to look at individuals' timetables to help with seeing what can be fitted in where. For example, once independent, if there is a half day free during the week this might be a good time to do shopping, better still would be to pick it up on the way home from somewhere else, thus avoiding a special 'shopping trip'. Everywhere will be less busy during the week and the precious weekend time can be preserved for nicer things.

Good routines will include coinciding chores and tasks; you can encourage clients to get into the habit of wiping down the work surface or cleaning the sink for example while they are boiling the kettle for a drink.

You can help individuals to create viable plans for routine and structure. However, the hardest part for you will be to enable them to realise that once the plan is in place it needs to be carried out in order for it to enjoy any sort of success.

Clearly, simple routine and structure can have a profound effect on how your clients will feel and a good typical daily routine would need to include most or all of the below.

Make bed

Put clothes away

Finish any study, work

Prepare bag for next day

Tidy up last thing at night

Get rid of rubbish

Switch off everything before going to bed

This is a very simple start but even this might seem quite daunting for somebody not used to it. You can help your clients get used to achieving a list like this before moving on and as they begin to get things under control, a few more tasks can be added. These can include:

Deal with post

Washing up

Preparing food

Locking up

A weekly routine might be:

Washing and drying laundry

Plan meals

Shopping list/Get shopping

Wipe inside of fridge

Check any study or work is up to date

Deal with outstanding post

Cleaning

This is an optimistic list of must-do's, the good thing is that most of them only take a few minutes. You will achieve a lot if you can get your clients to think in terms of little and often, this way nothing gets a chance to build up and mundane chores will be under control. The pay-off for individuals will be experiencing what it really feels like to take pride in where they live, knowing that it is all down to them.

Cleanliness

Cleaning has got to be high priority where routines are concerned. Keeping your home clean is a huge subject and there are some fantastic books available explaining how best to do it. For my book though, we are going to cover simple basics that you can pass on to your clients to help them understand the importance of keeping a home clean and to encourage the habit of doing it regularly.

A basic fact your clients will need to know is where bacteria lurks within the home. It thrives in any of the following.

Washing-up cloths

Beds

Towels

Tea towels

Germs live in their millions in damp washing-up cloths. This can be kept under control by using a brush and a scourer to wash up instead of a cloth. If a washing up sponge is used it needs to dry out between uses and be got rid of after a week to ten days. Packs of inexpensive cleaning cloths from supermarkets are good for general cleaning so that after cleaning bins, floors or work surfaces with disinfectant or bleach, they can be thrown away.

Beds are another potential breeding ground for bacteria. To maximise hygiene in bed linen you can encourage the use of a flat sheet folded in half under the sheet used for sleeping on or, if finances allow, a mattress protector.

All bed linen, towels and tea towels, need to be washed on a hot setting to kill germs and bacteria.

Your clients will also need to keep the bathroom clean. The sink, toilet bowl and floor need to be wiped with disinfectant every two to three days and bleached at night. Toothbrushes need to be changed regularly too.

Clearly opening your clients' minds to the importance of a clean home will be an important part of your work around routine and structure. However, you will be underpinning all of this by guiding them to the understanding that they are of value and so it should follow that their home is too. An individual's environment and safety is important, but the main investment your clients will be making through these routine cleaning tasks won't only be in their accommodation, they will be investing fully in themselves.

When and how your clients sort their routines will depend very much on individual preferences. Remember, whatever they decide is fine, with your help they will be able to create a calm and safe environment with nobody in charge but themselves.

1.8 The Safe in 'Safe Haven'

Creating a safe place isn't something that will just happen, you can enable your clients to achieve this for themselves by passing on some basic information. There are practical things to do as well as other more subtle things which will help towards feeling emotionally and psychologically safe.

Whether a move is imminent or not, it is never too early to start some simple involvement with safety around a home. Instilling a sense of responsibility right now will provide a heightened awareness after moving.

Sometimes a few simple changes can make all the difference when it comes to being able to completely relax at home. You will need to use your skills to discuss and discover what it is that enables your clients to feel safe. This work is important; when an individual talks to you about what they need to feel safe, it may well be the first time they will have recognised it for themselves.

There are a number of things that will make any of us feel safe and the list below covers some of them, your clients may well add many more.

Doors locked

Phones unplugged or switched off

Computer switched off

Being alone

Being with someone who can be trusted

Have music on

Be in silence

Television or radio on or off

Access to food and drink

Comfortable clothes

Privacy

Warmth

Despite some of these things appearing to be very simple, some of them could be quite difficult for an individual to acknowledge, and even more difficult to implement. The reasons for this might be complex but your clients will only succeed in independence if they can truthfully accept what their needs are and then be brave enough to act on this knowledge. Some of the reasons clients might not want to acknowledge what they really need are below.

- The need to be alone. This could promote anxiety about missing out on what is going on with other people.

- The need to switch off phones. This could lead to fear that they will miss an important call.

- The need for silence. Silence can lead to uncontrolled thoughts, often these are painful or upsetting.

Your clients may find it incredibly hard to acknowledge to themselves, let alone to you, that doing any of these things would be in their best interests. Your job around this issue is to help them to take their needs seriously and to enable them to see that anything else will be a barrier to creating the environment they need. You are the one to assure them that as soon as they start to do this, people around them will start taking them seriously too.

Once your clients have come up with some suggestions about what makes them feel safe, they can start to get used to the idea that there needs to be some significant changes in their lives. However, habits are a bit like clutter; somehow they feel safe, even when they are not helping. As with the clutter though, it is the safety of not changing anything that provides that feeling. A significant change like switching off a phone or a computer, even for short periods of time can be quite daunting and a very powerful exercise in control. If an individual gradually gets used to the experience of quiet and safety, they will get used to feelings of control in their own space.

Things will need to start gently. It takes time to get used to any change and the fears your clients may have around missing important calls will make it difficult to deal with. Television, radio or music probably provides a welcome background that can help to prevent deep thoughts or feelings. When you begin your work on this I would suggest turning everything off, one evening a week for just an hour or so to see how it feels. As everything becomes more familiar you could try to introduce a routine, say, by 8 o'clock, three or four evenings a week there is a sort of close down with as much as is comfortably possible, switched off.

Being in a quiet place might feel very strange, and even though it is desired, it can also be potentially frightening. Your task here is to use a working session to share the experience of quiet, encourage the use of use a journal to record thoughts and feelings. Individuals may well be inspired to write down other things they need within the home that will add emotional comfort or value.

Only your clients can decide how far they want to go and how often. Television can be invasive and mind numbing but, it can also be an amazingly valuable thing with great potential to enhance everyday life. The message here is not that technology is bad or wrong, it is about your clients understanding what will enable them to feel safe and then being free enough to make the choices. What you can do is support individuals by helping them to explore other ways to spend time, and take it very slowly.

Gradually, as you work through my book the confidence of individuals will grow, they will feel much more comfortable about not depending on old unhelpful habits. They will begin to see and understand that they are able to create a safe environment which underpins who they are.

Fire

Knowledge about the prevention of fire is an absolute must for keeping a home safe. Clients moving into their own homes can be at particular risk because there are so many extra things to deal with at this time. If you take individuals through all the basic routines and practices below they will be adequately prepared to keep themselves safe.

- Switch off all electrical appliances when not in use

- Avoid overloading electrical sockets with extension leads and extra plugs

- Make sure all cigarette ends are properly out

- Know how to test and change batteries in smoke detectors

- Know how to test and change batteries in carbon monoxide detector

- Safe use of candles. Never place them near curtains or on low tables.

- Close all internal doors at night, this will help to delay the spread of fire

- Do not throw water on hot fat

- Know how to use a domestic fire extinguisher

- Know how and when to use a fire blanket

The work you do on these simple and basic things must not be underestimated, you are setting in place safe practices which will be used confidently in the future.

Intruders

Worrying about intruders in the home is not something anybody wants to be spending time on. Below are some basic strategies to take some of the fear of intruders away.

- Ensure all outside windows and doors have working locks

- Windows should have catches that cannot be opened from the outside

- If sleeping on the ground floor, close the window before going to bed or going out

- Have chain locks on external doors

- Keep doors locked, even when at home

- Have two sets of keys, if one gets lost this prevents having to break in

- Have identity tag on keys, no name or address, just telephone number

- Leave light on, curtains closed if going out

- Let somebody know if going away, they can keep an eye on things

If possible the individuals you work with should be given responsibility for some of these things before moving. Knowing they can do their best to prevent an intrusion happening will help allay the fear of it.

Health/First Aid

Project:

First Aid Box

Within the realms of keeping safe comes first aid and medication. Every home needs to have some sort of provision for off-colour days or emergencies.

This is a project which relates to maturity and will be something to work with when your clients can be responsible for keeping medication safe. I am assuming they are in good health.

Creating a first aid or medication box is a good opportunity to create something very personal. The container itself can reflect interests or preferences in style and it doesn't have to be purpose built, anything that appeals which is large enough to hold the necessary items is fine. When it is eventually in the home, just like the memory box, it will contain something of the individual, thus adding tremendous emotional value.

Some suggestions of what could go in to your clients' first aid or medication box are below.

Pain relief

Plasters

Antiseptic cream

Cream for burns, bites, stings

Sun protection

Relief from flu symptoms

Cough medicine

Sore throat sweets

Chest rub, vapour

Thermometer

Essential oils

Cream for bruising

Remedies for stomach upsets

Telephone numbers of doctor and hospital

We all feel better if we know we have got everything we need in case we are not well but a strong message can be sent to your clients through this. It is especially important that they feel valued, not only by you and other people around them, but also by themselves. Organising and preparing a medication box is a strong self-affirming message, during the time they spend on it they will be acknowledging their own worth.

It will be down to you to help individuals understand the importance of maintaining health and how responsibly medication needs to be treated. Your clients need to respect what is in the box and keep it safe. They will also need to remember to register with a new doctor and dentist after moving.

To keep healthy we all need to take regular exercise which works up a sweat at least three times a week for around twenty-five minutes at a time.

Apart from exercise simple things like getting out into the fresh air for at least fifteen minutes a day helps the body to produce vitamin D. This is not sunbathing, just exposing some skin will be sufficient.

Health is not all about the physical, your clients' state of mind or mental health underpins who they are and how they will cope with life. Being happy is good for us and contagious too, so encourage individuals to have fun, make friends, and have a laugh on a regular basis. This will release endorphins into the system and they will feel better about everything.

Being safe can have many connotations and keeping safe

from ill health is crucial in helping your clients' lives to run smoothly. This does not mean hiding away from germs and bugs, some exposure to these things are important to help build up the immune system. Diet also plays a major role in keeping healthy and therefore safe.

A truly safe haven needs to be the place where individuals can completely relax. It is important they understand how the efforts they are making towards creating their safe space reflects their own personalities. You are the person to help them stay focused on this.

1.9 Boundaries

There are many ways that the peace of your clients' homes can be disrupted. To create a truly safe place to live it is crucial for some boundaries to be in place.

A boundary is a dividing line between what is acceptable and what is not and in the context of home, boundaries are not only concerned with what other people might do, they are also very much concerned with what your clients may or may not do. Personal boundaries need to be in place with regard to self-discipline, providing protection from triggered habits or behaviour.

Unfortunately, even when they are in place, boundaries can be difficult to maintain. You are in the position to offer your clients practical help and support in not only exploring what they should be, but also how to keep them intact.

During your work on this subject you may find yourself up against some real resistance. This is a difficult issue for anyone to tackle and your clients may not be able to, or even want to recognise the types of boundaries they really need to put in place. However, as you continue your work a gradual understanding will evolve about how boundaries can enhance life and help to keep a home secure.

We all have all sorts of individual boundaries in place and the purpose of these is to keep us physically, emotionally and psychologically safe. Very often though, we only become aware of them when they are breached, whether knowingly or unwittingly.

Some of the reasons your clients' personal boundaries might get breached are below.

- When people don't know each other very well it is difficult to understand where personal boundaries are, these are not something we usually announce to others.

- People often talk about subjects openly without realising another person may have strong feelings about it.

- Each of us will have a different set of boundaries. However, we tend to make the assumption that everybody else's boundaries are the same as ours, this can lead to all sorts of confusion and offence.

To complicate things further, there are also different types of boundaries.

Firstly, there are outer boundaries, these are about what goes on in the immediate space around us, generally thought to be about an arm's length away from our bodies. If somebody gets into this space it can make us feel uncomfortable or even angry and we would instinctively take a step back.

Occasionally the person invading our space won't pick up on this signal and will just move forward towards us again, this is the time when we need to be strong enough to defend our boundary.

As with the breaching of many other boundaries, stepping

into somebody's personal space can be an indicator about the relationship; the person moving in or breaking the boundary is demanding control and will retain it if it is not addressed. Although your clients may not want to analyse the psychological dynamics, they will certainly feel them.

Boundaries need to be flexible too. With regard to personal space, if your client is feeling low, they may not want any close contact with anybody else and their boundary may extend to several rooms. If they are feeling alright, or have a very close bond with somebody then they may decide that no space at all is needed.

We are conditioned to adjust our boundaries according to our circumstances. For example, a complete stranger may need to be well within our personal space if we were travelling on a crowded train or sitting in a theatre. In these circumstances we would overcome our instinctive feelings.

Another example of an outer boundary would be somebody taking something that didn't belong to them without permission. It could be anything, large or small, the impact would be the same. If your clients experience anything like this, they would need to be strong enough to keep the boundary in place by challenging the behaviour.

As well as outer boundaries, there are also inner boundaries. For many reasons these are much more difficult to identify and to keep intact. Setting inner boundaries is like creating a barrier of protection around emotions, they are about our personal fears, anxieties and concerns over issues that we may prefer to keep to ourselves. Your clients, understandably, may be reluctant to talk about these or even think about them in any depth.

It is not difficult to see then how individuals can be inadvertently offended and a whole chain reaction of emotions set off because they haven't thought through and recognised the need to create a boundary around an issue they feel strongly about.

Boundaries can only be set when the need for them has been recognised. To do this your clients will need to acknowledge honestly how they feel about many subjects and you will undoubtedly find that many of them will find this difficult.

Some of the reasons your clients might want to avoid the issue of setting boundaries are below.

Feelings might be seen as weaknesses

The belief that they are not worthy of boundaries

Feeling they have to please everybody

The need to be accepted

Your clients' boundaries will be built on the control needed around their feelings, body, personal space, thoughts and beliefs.

Set out below is a list of questions you can use to initiate discussions; because of the probing nature of these, your work will need to be slow and gentle. They can be used as one-off questions or one can lead straight to another, depending on the answers.

- Do you find yourself ignoring what you want or feel so you can please other people?

- Does the way other people treat you make you the person you are?

- Do you feel guilty if you say 'no'?

- Do you find it difficult to disagree with others, even if you feel strongly?

- Can you say 'no' without an explanation?

- Do you feel under pressure to give more than you are able?

- Do you find yourself taking more than you need?

The purpose of these discussions is to raise an individual's self-awareness, to help them to see their own attitudes and behaviour. Once this begins to happen they will be able to take steps to protect themselves.

Work on this subject may well be a slow and challenging process but completely worthwhile. When an individual has clear, self-imposed boundaries that they understand and respect they will have real choices for themselves which will hold no consequences.

Below are some examples of typical personal boundaries your clients may need to put in place.

- Time spent on computer, games, television, phone

- Spending money

- Frequency of seeing a new friend

- How late in the evening to take a phone call or visit

- Time spent alone, too much or too little

- Who comes into the home

- Not being humiliated in any way

- Who to give contact details to and when

- When and where not to give or take judgement or criticism

- When or where not to help a friend – homework, money, covering for

- Personal privacy, space

- When or where not to give an opinion
- When or where not to take an opinion

There are various ways that your clients' boundaries can be breached, the list below will help you to highlight some of them to bring about awareness, therefore reducing vulnerability.

Phone or text

E-mail

Receiving too much attention

Having something 'borrowed' on a regular basis

Receiving uninvited guests at home

Over or under eating

Receiving uninvited opinions

Uncontrolled spending

If appropriate boundaries are not in place, there can be a variety of consequences, the list below illustrates some of these but they may well experience others too.

Inappropriate contact with friends or family

Emotional upset

Debt

Unwelcome visitors

Taking or making calls at inappropriate times

Disruption to plans affecting work or college

Being bullied

Feeling hurt or used

A boundary has been crossed when a person begins to feel uncomfortable, this is the time to identify the need. When setting boundaries individuals need to keep them positive and be flexible; we all change and grow, boundaries need to change too.

Once a boundary is in place, your clients need to be able to verbalise their feelings in their own language, it's no good trying to learn a script, it won't be genuine and will lack clarity.

The list below illustrates some of the ways your clients can protect a boundary.

- Say what they feel
- Change the subject being discussed
- Physically move away
- Avoid smiling
- Avoid apologising
- Feel confident about the right to have boundaries
- Get used to taking responsibility for them
- Give boundaries priority
- Avoid trying to please
- 'No' doesn't need any support or justification
- Be flexible and aware of what is going on
- Get help

Boundaries help prevent all sorts of manipulation by others and when they are known, they send a clear signal.

However, even with the strategies shown here there are no guarantees and your clients will have to face the fact that they can't always choose what happens. Individuals can't force their boundaries onto other people if they won't accept them. Occasionally they will just have to take a strong stance such as stop the conversation or move out of a situation completely.

It is crucial that your clients work out for themselves what their own personal boundaries are, they will have no commitment to them if somebody else has decided what they should be. When they have worked some of them out you can encourage them to create a list of what they are and display them where they can be seen.

Boundaries are something that we all have to work hard with whatever our age or experience, there will always be a situation which can invade our personal comfort zone in one way or another. It is crucial therefore that your clients understand that when this happens, they have not failed in any way, this is just a fact of life.

As individuals gradually get used to defending their boundaries successfully they will become more comfortable with the whole issue and will start to enjoy increased self-confidence and feelings of self-worth. A confident person instils confidence in others and your clients will notice the respect they are gaining from people around them and may well find themselves inspiring their peers.

1.10 Body Language

A real home can provide foundations and safety within your clients' lives but anything troublesome that happens in the outside world will inevitably be brought back to disrupt the peace that has been so hard to create.

Body language can be used as a self-protecting tool but if not used appropriately, in social situations it can send powerful messages of the wrong kind to the wrong people in a matter of seconds. It could be easy for your clients to inadvertently give the impression that their home is open house to anybody who feels like dropping by. Before they know where they are, they can find themselves in difficult to handle relationships that they never intended to happen.

There are various basic ways of using body language that will help to keep your clients safe.

Avoid eye contact

Do not give out contact details too readily

Dress appropriately

Try not to smile too much

Avoid appearing submissive. This can be done by individuals making themselves as high and wide as possible, standing if necessary, speaking clearly and confidently and holding the head up straight.

In order to use body language to their advantage, your clients will firstly need to consider how much of themselves they want to give away. This may well be different for males and females.

A female may want to feel attractive and know that she can attract a male she is interested in. However, she will also still want to retain the option of pulling back.

A male might be more interested in gaining respect from his peers. Whatever the reasons for attracting attention, if he doesn't have enough information about what he is saying, he cannot be completely in control of events.

Body language can easily and sometimes inadvertently

send the message that an individual is looking for attention and below are a few examples.

Wearing 'on trend' clothes

Displaying and playing with objects such as phones

Well-groomed and styled hair

Make-up, perfume, aftershave

Wearing conspicuous jewellery

Showing flesh

Having own transport

I think it is fairly safe to assume that most of us have done or still do some of these things and it's hardly fair to say that we shouldn't because we might get the wrong sort of attention. The key for remaining safe is to develop a sense of discernment. You will be trying to help your clients to develop their instincts or gut feelings about who may be genuinely interested in them as individuals or who will want to take advantage of them in some way. This is no easy task, it takes confidence and inner strength on the part of the client to acknowledge that somebody might only be talking to them because they want to steal their phone – or worse.

The people you work with may be keen to gain friends and so could easily lose sight of some of the obvious ways to tell if somebody is genuine or not. This is even more likely to be the case when an amount of trust begins to form between them, your clients will become more blinkered and unable to detect possible deceit. It is very difficult for any of us to acknowledge that one of our friends is not what they might seem.

Below are some examples of signals that might be sent out by somebody who is not genuine. Your clients need to be watching out for these in people they get involved with.

Over anxious behaviour, fidgeting

Lack of eye contact

Too much eye contact

Blinking a lot

Forced smile

Lots of talking but not much information

Not listening

Inappropriate touching

If you can encourage your clients to be open to the idea that not everybody they meet will be what they might seem, this will be a big step. They will be able to take a step back and listen to their instincts, this will provide them with choices, and if they begin to feel uncomfortable in any way, they can choose to take more control of the situation.

Your clients may well be making themselves vulnerable by unintentionally sending out the wrong signals. Below are some examples of what a male or a female might inadvertently be doing.

Hair flicking or running hands through hair

Exchanging glances to catch somebody's eye

Holding eye contact for longer than usual

Fluttering eye lashes

Pouting or licking lips

Smiling at somebody unknown

Crossing and uncrossing legs

Sitting legs astride and leaning towards unknown person

Sitting too close to somebody unknown

Clearly the list can go on but these are the very basic and more commonly used signals that will attract attention. Your clients may use them without even thinking about it. It is your job to enable them to understand the messages they may be sending and to make them aware that to give themselves a proper choice in who they start a relationship of any kind with, they need to be aware of what they are doing.

It can be very difficult for anybody to completely control who visits or phones them but if you provide your clients with some basic knowledge about body language and how to present themselves safely to the world, it will go a long way to keeping them and their home safe.

1.11 Relationships

At the same time your clients are learning awareness to body language they will also be learning how to manage their relationships whether they be close or distant. Managing relationships is a complex and sometimes difficult thing to do but you can offer practical help and support which will show individuals how to deal with the people they are involved with.

Many of your clients may be unable to acknowledge whether their relationships are good for them or not. They may also be maintaining some of them for the wrong reasons.

We all need to feel loved and wanted and it is this need that can cause any of us to become vulnerable with regard to relationships. Enabling your clients to recognise what might be an unhealthy situation could make a significant difference, both now and in the future, to how they live their lives and therefore how they run their homes.

Once your clients have developed an emotional bond with somebody, or have always known that bond to be there, it is incredibly difficult for them to step back and look objectively at what is really happening. Their attachment could get in the way and blur all the issues.

None of us are born with the inner knowledge on how to run successful relationships, we learn this from each other and through experience. It will be part of your job, while using my book, to try to break through any barriers your clients may have and open their minds to seeing their relationships as they really are, for good or for bad.

Below are some of the positive aspects your clients can expect from a healthy relationship.

It will…

Help them as individuals

Enrich their lives

Make them better people

Bring joy

Encourage belief in themselves

Allow the development of trust

Provide evidence that they can be loved

Allow them to love themselves

Below are some of the not so positive aspects clients could expect to experience if they are in an unhealthy relationship.

None of the above

Feeling uncomfortable, sad or afraid

Being controlled in one or more ways

Being told how to dress, think or feel

Fear of other person's temper or dark moods

Use of physical, verbal or emotional pressure

Many of these things are difficult to see from the outside, the manipulation by one person over the other may well succeed in hiding them. Your clients have plenty to deal with in their lives and if they are in unhealthy relationships as well, the pressure of all of this could prove to be a very heavy burden.

There are many reasons why individuals might want to stay in an unhealthy relationship, below are some of the things they might feel.

Fear of –

Being alone

Reaction from the other person

The unknown

Any change

Has a strong need to feel loved

If an individual is used to having bad feelings around a relationship these become familiar and so feel safe, even leading to an amount of security.

This subject is sensitive but, you are in a position to develop your clients' awareness of what is actually happening between themselves and the people around them. You will be able to show how to use the evidence shown within a relationship to help with assessing whether it is healthy or not.

The questions below will help you initiate discussions about how current relationships really feel. Because of the nature of the way you can work through my book, you will be able to broach these issues in an informal way when opportunities arise. Your clients will soon learn that being honest about feelings will provide the evidence to see what is actually happening.

- How do you feel after being with …?

- What sort of mood are you in when you have been away from …?

- How do you feel when you say goodbye to …?

- How do you feel when you know you are going to see …?

- What decisions do you make with … in mind?

- Are you free to say what you really feel when you are with …?

- Do you feel guilty if you do or don't do things to please …?

- Are you able to say no when you want to when you are with …?

You can encourage individuals to use the above as a self-questioning strategy themselves. They can then soon begin to assess not only the relationships they are already in, but potential relationships too, before they get in too deep.

If your clients recognise that they are in relationships that they would be better off without, there are some simple practical ways to ease themselves away.

Be out of reach – switch off mobile devices

Don't answer the door

Don't take anything valuable out

Be busy, make plans – avoid always being available

Avoid being alone with the other person

Explain

Gradually, as your clients get used to this questioning and assessing, their belief in their own judgement will grow. Over a period of time they will come to understand that the outcome of changing or ending a bad relationship, however this might be done, will eventually feel more comfortable than actually being in it as it is. Only by gaining this type of control over their lives can they really protect their home environment.

Assertiveness

With regard to keeping the home safe, your clients need to feel they are strong enough to choose to either ask somebody to leave or to prevent them from coming in. Everybody needs to be in a position where they can decide who comes into their home, whether it is through technology or the door.

As with many other skills, assertiveness isn't something that comes naturally. Once your clients are confident with being assertive they will have a starting point for actually knowing when and how to take more control in life. Individuals need to be able to say 'no' at appropriate times without fear of recrimination or guilt, this means being able to take their own feelings seriously and acting upon them. This will become easier for them as they realise and understand that you are taking them seriously too.

If an individual is afraid to say 'no' and stand by it, there will be a variety of uncomfortable consequences to deal with including the build-up of anger and resentment because of feelings of frustration. Below are some of the reasons why people are not assertive enough.

Fear of not be liked anymore

Feelings of guilt

Not wanting to be left out

Fear of getting hurt

Afraid of hurting somebody

Although assertiveness is not being aggressive, there are times when an aggressive response is completely appropriate. If a client is being assaulted for example, then an amount of aggression is fine. Generally speaking though, assertiveness is used to deal with the more subtle ways people have of getting you to do something you don't really want to do.

Becoming more assertive will inevitably mean changing some patterns of behaviour. Many of your clients will feel uncomfortable with this. You will need to reassure them that everybody feels like this and that once they experience the benefits of assertiveness these feelings will fade.

Assertiveness creates choice; your clients will soon begin to understand that they can take control of a situation, thereby reducing feelings of helplessness or inadequacy. By learning a new way of behaving they will start to enjoy being in a position where they don't have to put up with unwanted demands, they will be in control of what they do or don't do.

These are some of the positive feelings your clients will begin to experience as they become more assertive.

More…

Self-confidence

Pride

Freedom

Motivation and drive

Self-respect

Respect from others

There are lots of ways of saying 'no' without actually using the word and if your clients are to be successful, they need to discover a way to say this comfortably. It would be no good learning parrot-fashion a selection of assertive phrases if they are genuinely not comfortable with using them. When the time comes, they will just cave in.

One of the simplest ways to show this is to use mini role play sessions.

As an example, we will assume there is a friend who keeps 'borrowing' small amounts of money and not paying it back. A technique which doesn't involve saying 'no' is this.

As soon as the friend approaches, your client should stand up straight and smile. When the friend is close enough the client should pre-empt the situation by saying, "I know why you have come over, but unfortunately I haven't got any money with me today." They should then smile again and walk away.

This sounds a simple enough exercise but playing it out for real might not be so easy. You can help by practising it with your clients. As individuals get used to hearing themselves speak, discovering how it feels when they move assertively, as well as your response to this, any initial embarrassment will fade and they will start to feel at ease and more confident about it.

Another possible situation is an unwelcome guest coming to the door. Individuals need to be able to cope confidently with this to be sure that only people they want in their homes actually come in.

Your client should answer the door and smile, this gives a mixed message to the other person which provides a couple of seconds for your client to take control and say clearly that they have plans for the afternoon/evening. Then, smiling again, close the door.

By role playing with your clients you will enable them to become used to hearing themselves use particular phrases and words. This will give them the confidence to use these in real situations, putting them in charge of a situation.

Clearly there are many complicated underlying reasons why your clients might be afraid of losing or alienating people around them, this often results in giving in to their demands. The most important thing you can show somebody with regard to keeping the home safe is that the control has got to come from themselves. The people making the demands are not going to change, while they are getting what they want they are going to stay the same, the situation will only change if your clients choose to send different messages.

Sometimes, just knowing they have the ability to change a situation will provide enormous confidence and alter the way an individual behaves generally, this in itself will make them less vulnerable.

The work you can do in a situation like this is invaluable. As you show genuine concern and support for your clients you will see them flourish and a mutual trust between you will build up. They will also learn by their experience with you, what a trusting and supportive relationship feels like.

1.12 Facing Fear

The prospect of setting up a new home would be daunting for anybody. For your clients, with their varying needs and experiences, it could be an experience fraught with fear. This section looks at how individuals can recognise and start to deal with some of the fear attached to a major life change such as a move to independence.

It is true to say that all of us experience fear at times, below are some of the more common ones.

The loss of something important

Failure

Being ill

Change

Being alone

Making decisions

Getting old

Natural disasters

For your clients, who are going through the anxieties associated with a major change, you can probably add several more such as

How will I pay the rent?

Who will wake me up?

What if I miss work or college?

What am I going to eat?

What about my friends or family?

Can I budget successfully?

These are all internal fears and your clients will need to recognise which ones are specifically affecting them before you can do anything to help. It can be very hard to admit to living with deep-rooted fears, it is therefore not unusual for internal fears to dictate the path of a client's life as they try to accommodate them.

From your perspective, to think this through honestly about yourself and then be open about the fears you have around some issues, might be quite difficult. Take a few minutes to try it to see how it feels. For your clients it will be very, very difficult. Using empathy and understanding it is your role to help and to enable this to happen. Only then will individuals really see how these fears play out in life and how they might have affected decisions made in the past. If they are not recognised, they will continue to have an impact on future decisions.

The fears above are what we call everyday fears. These are about things which may or may not happen to any one of us. Other everyday fears are built around things we have to do and might include any of the below.

Driving, parking

Going to work, college

Making decisions

Meeting deadlines

Meeting new people

Making small talk

These 'doing' fears are called action fears and it's not difficult to see that each one of them is loaded with possible disasters. Once your clients start to identify them they will see them everywhere and begin to notice how much they affect their lives.

It might be quite a slow process and you will need to be patient, allowing time for thoughts to filter through but gradually, individuals will begin to realise that fear is an element in life which will not be helping.

Although the fear in itself is not always significant enough to worry too much about, it is the related impact that it can have on life which needs to be looked at. For example, if somebody is always afraid of making a mistake, they will play everything safe, never pushing themselves too far, never looking at new or possibly more exciting ways of doing things. Fear is governing their life.

Fear can come into our lives in a variety of ways, the fears outlined above are about our situations, others can be about our inner selves, the list below shows that these are many and varied.

Dependency

Disapproval from others

Loss of identity

Being taken for granted

Being too vulnerable

Being rejected

Loving too much

Not being loved

Using just one from the list as an example, rejection, if your clients are afraid of this then it will colour their lives. Subconsciously they will try to avoid involvement with anything that might allow a situation to arise that will leave them open to being or feeling rejected. It can affect their ability to make deep and trusting relationships and on a simpler level can affect whether or not they smile at the cashier in the local garage.

By allowing fear to rule, and by protecting themselves in this way, individuals can actually cut themselves off from who they really are, or all the possibilities of who they could be.

The bottom line with all fear, whatever it is about, is that it gives you the feeling that you won't be able to cope with whatever life presents to you. This is actually not the case and your clients need to be aware of, and in control of, any fears they may have if a new life, establishing a new home, is to be a long-term success.

Fear makes us want to close down, shut the world out, disengage, but if your clients can remove this powerful negative force from their world, they would begin to open up to life and flourish. They would be confident in knowing that whatever happens, they will be strong enough to cope.

Use the examples below for dealing with fear by gradually introducing them into your work. They will provide another opportunity for your clients to tune into thoughts and identify the negative ones. These are the thoughts that tell us things like: "I'm never going to find a job, my whole life will be ruined." The resulting emotion coming out of this thought is fear, fear of being on the scrap heap, never having enough money, not being as good as everybody else.

You can help your clients to identify a thought which creates fear, then to practice substituting it for a positive thought which will help bring about feelings of calmness and control.

This is no easy task for you. Firstly there is the hurdle of clients recognising and acknowledging their inner negative self-talk, and then the work involved in the substitutions.

Working with your clients this way will be time consuming

and you will need plenty of patience but take heart, this job is one of the most worthwhile you can do with somebody, showing how to start to control fear will create an outlook on life which will bring about a real sense of freedom.

Examples of swapping negative thoughts with positive ones might be:

I will never be able to manage everything on my own, I'm just not good enough:

Change to:

Being on my own might be hard to begin with but I know I can do it, and I will keep on trying until it works out.

Or:

I know I will be late, then I will get into trouble and lose my job.

Change to:

I know I am often late, I need to allow more time for things and plan ahead, I know I can do this.

Although they come frequently, your clients may not recognise how powerful negative thoughts are and how much influence they can have. However, instead of being at the mercy of these thoughts that can deliver fear in huge quantities, once tuned in to them, your clients will be able to develop new ways of thinking that will reflect the feelings needed to change their outlook on life.

You can suggest that individuals test themselves every now and again by taking a risk and smiling at the cashier. If she doesn't smile back, the new inner dialogue should be that she is just thinking of something else, her response is not personal. Strategies for overcoming any fear can be learnt, and when thinking is reshaped, the increased confidence and trust in themselves that they will experience will provide individuals with the ability to seriously reshape their lives.

Unfortunately, fear is a fact of life and it will always be with us, but once your clients have learnt that it can't be excluded from life, they can begin to accept it and learn ways to conquer its limiting affects. A comforting thought is that we are all in the same boat, if your clients are feeling fear, it would be good for you to remind them that they can safely assume everybody else in their situation is feeling it too.

The message you will be putting across is that being afraid of doing something doesn't mean you don't do it. If you are determined to face your fears then you need to meet them head on.

An idea like this could make someone incredibly anxious, but it will be reassuring for the people you work with to know that this anxiety is short lived and that it is much easier in the long run to confront their source of unease than to live with the continual nightmare of what it brings. Only when the very thing creating the fear has been faced will things start to improve. Your clients will find that facing a potentially traumatic situation and overcoming it will boost confidence and have a liberating effect; the tables will have been turned on their relationship with fear and they will be in control.

If you encourage your clients to face this work confidently they will learn from experience that it is possible to successfully deal with all that fear can present to them and transform the way they approach life.

1.13 For you – listening skills

Spending time talking and listening to the clients in your care is one of the best ways to help them through the many issues raised within my book. Showing you are really interested will help to increase their sense of self-worth as well as affirming their whole sense of being.

Without needing any verbal acknowledgement, individuals will know you are investing time and energy into them and will gradually begin to understand that this is because they are actually worth this effort.

Below are some of the things you can do to ensure you are a good listener.

- Accept the person speaking, be unconditional in this regardless of your client's views and opinions.

- Give full attention, show you are doing this by remaining still while listening, give eye contact and have open body language.

- Be encouraging, respond to what is being said by nodding or saying yes occasionally.

- Have empathy, put yourself in the position of your clients, try to understand their feelings.

- Allow silences.

- Try to have the ability to look beyond the words. Is there something more to what is being said? Are your clients 'talking around' a bigger issue?

- Have the ability to read body language.

- Avoid interrupting, allow people to take their time.

- Reflect on the conversation as you go along, this ensures

you both understand what is being said and your clients are reassured that you have been listening.

Your aim in improving your listening skills is to enable your clients to express themselves freely and confidently with you.

A poor listener may display some of the actions below. Try to avoid as many as possible!

- Poor body language, not giving appropriate eye contact, looking bored or disinterested, fidgeting, sitting too close or too far away, turning away when the person is speaking.

- Having interruptions to your conversation, people coming in and going out of the room, telephones ringing.

- Allowing your clients to be uncomfortable, too warm or too cold, using uncomfortable chairs.

- Showing insincerity, boredom or prejudice.

The importance of actively listening to your clients cannot be overstated. My book is built around communication between you so it is imperative that as much as possible of what your clients say is picked up and worked with.

CONCEPT TWO

YOUR PERSONAL HISTORY MAKES YOU WHO YOU ARE – RECOGNISE IT IN YOUR HOME AND CREATE A TRUE SENSE OF BELONGING

"Past, present and future are linked inseparably
in the way we think and act."
Michael Jacobs

2.1 Personal History – Cultural Identity

Your job in relation to my book is to enable your clients firstly, to identify aspects of their personal history which have contributed to their cultural identity, and secondly how to interweave these aspects into a home in a way that will provide a sense of self-worth and belonging.

Research has shown that individuals coming out of a supported living environment struggle to maintain their lives successfully long-term in the accommodation they are provided with. Over one fifth of young people leaving the care system become homeless within two years of becoming independent.[4]

As your clients move to independent living, their health and well-being will be paramount. Using personal history will help to underpin the foundations of who they are and reinforce the idea that they are truly within the margins of everyday life. In other words, they fit in.

The people you work with are complex, on the one hand they need to be seen and respected for their individuality while on the other, they don't want to be on the outside and therefore treated as different. Pulling threads of personal history together and expressing it within a home will not only enable individuals to see themselves in a positive way but will enable them to have some control over how other people see them.

The way the homes of your clients evolve might appear to an outsider to be a random collection of unrelated items, but the reality will be a positive representation of their life so far. Their homes will be constructed through the inner feelings that have developed whilst being shaped by a mixture of influences.

Identity is an individual thing and is one of those areas that can seem confusing and daunting for any of us as we try to work out where we are with it. It is likely that your clients will see their pasts in a negative light and could easily be limited by it. They may also try to avoid acknowledging it altogether.

Our personal history and cultural identity is created by the influence of the people who contributed to our upbringing and through the structure of our day-to-day life. It doesn't matter if the people you work with have experienced a wide range of differing cultural backgrounds or known just one. When it comes to their own homes, there may be some traditions they will want to take with them, some they will want to leave

---

[4] *Understanding Youth: Perspectives, Identities and Practices*, p.300, Ed. Mary Jane Kehily

behind and some new ones they will create for themselves.

Specific activities or interests we have had also contribute to our cultural identity, so do the special people we had in our lives who really cared about us. All of these aspects of the time your clients were growing up, and beyond, can be used to enhance the future.

The thought of living independently with the prospect of so many hidden unknowns looming would be frightening for any of us. The individuals you work with may well feel confused by the strong feelings they have around the emotional and social implications of the complex mix of their roots. Even though it is inevitable, you may find that they are reluctant to even think about moving and, when it eventually happens, they may well go through a sort of cultural bereavement. This will be brought about by the sense of loss they will feel regarding the support they have been receiving. This can be a lonely ordeal. All sorts of insecurities and worries can come to the surface as the familiarity of the social norms they have grown used to are taken away.

By using the home as a focus you can help your clients to think positively regarding the past, encouraging the brave step to explore the whole of it. You can help them to understand that if big chunks of the past are ignored, parts of who they really are can effectively be lost. When this happens, the smooth integration of the past with the present, something which is crucial if their new life is to be successful in the long run, is threatened.

Relating to the past in this way will be a gradual process and will need patience and sensitivity on your part. Although the aim is to explore all of it, you may find that a small and slow start will need to be good enough.

Through this second Concept you will be encouraging your clients to look positively at specifics and, as understanding of their history grows and confidence increases, they will be equipping themselves to overcome the feelings of disengagement and alienation that so many people feel about their new accommodation. Individuals will eventually begin to develop belief in themselves and their ability to use their home as a means of expressing not only who they were, but who they are now and who they might be become.

2.2 Good Memories

To begin this project you will need to encourage your clients to look at specific memories they may want to use. You will need to bear in mind that although the big picture of an individual's history may consist of many life-changing situations, they will need to focus on just what they can use constructively within the home. Your responsibility will be to help them identify the events that built up the fabric of their everyday life, the smaller experiences that brought short bursts of pleasure or joy on a regular basis.

Smaller doesn't mean less important. These sometimes 'run of the mill' pastimes or interests will have undoubtedly played a strong part in creating an identity and making an individual the person they are today. For example, they may have loved kicking a football around a back garden or swimming or dancing or cycling. They might also have enjoyed something less physical like reading a certain magazine, watching a particular television programme or learning to play a musical instrument. What it was doesn't matter, the memory of it can be used to personalise their home.

Discovering for themselves the importance and value of these times will help to consolidate the life your clients have had so far and can be used to tell their story within the home. This creates something tangible, something to be seen and used every day as well as providing a supportive and nurturing environment. The importance of your clients' cultural journeys cannot be overestimated and their homes are where it can be explored and displayed freely.

As you work on this, individuals will gradually become more self-assured and able to express their history in any way they choose. For example, if they were close to somebody who worked on the railway they might decide to hang up a picture of a train. A client's history belongs only to them and they don't need to explain or justify it. You or I might see a picture of a train, your clients would see a whole range of memories, experiences and emotions pulling strands of their life together and helping to create a home filled with warmth and depth.

Remember that before starting on any journey into the past there needs to be some preparation for the impact it may have. Even when recalling something positive, it is possible that this could be related in some way to other experiences so, as your clients relive the good memories, these may be accompanied by a mixture of other, less welcome ones. If this happens, you can encourage them to take a step back and, when they are ready, they can take time to think of less entangled situations.

Identifying things that your clients loved doing is the first place to start, they can then begin to work on projects that will incorporate these into a home. Later when they see the reminders of these times around them, they will experience positive feelings about their past day-to-day life, bringing them comfortably forward into the present day. This way, their homes won't be built on transient experiences such as one-off holidays or days out, it will consist of the solidity of the everyday.

Your clients are not limited to any number of memories, getting in touch with as much of their younger selves as possible will help them to see how they have moved on. The more they can bring from their past into the present, the better the end result will be.

Because I have no way of knowing what your clients will

come up with, I am going to use the example of kicking a football around to show how to incorporate an experience into a home.

Project:

Photo displays

Using the football scenario, there are many different ways of representing this. Your clients may have photographs of themselves with a ball or wearing a team kit which can be used. If they don't have photographs it might be possible to track some down, maybe from previous carers, parents or other relatives. If it's not possible to get pictures of actually playing football, it is worth thinking about other related things, like a photograph with a friend of the time, or a school picture. These too will evoke the memory.

We need to bear in mind that there is more to seeing an old photograph of yourself than just looking at the picture and dating it. Your clients may be surprised at what they can see and feel when they look closely and this may trigger memories of lots of other good things that were going on in their lives at the time. This is the whole point and a simple picture could prove to be a rich source of information that can be used to rekindle the past. However, they only need to use memories they are comfortable with so sometimes, it might not be the whole era they will want to recall, but just one tiny bit of it. If this is what an individual is comfortable with then this is what they need to do. Gradually, as time goes on, they may be able to look at a fuller picture.

So how can your clients look with fresh eyes at an old image? They will need to look closely at the picture, it will contain lots of clues to help them remember the time. If they scrutinise it they will see what the weather was like – was it summer or winter? They can also look at anybody else in the image – who are they? What can be seen in the background? Maybe it's a house – whose is it? Is it some other type of building? What went on there? Gradually the details will trickle back.

Individuals can look to see how they used to wear their hair, were they tall for their age, or short, how did this make them feel, and so on. As they allow themselves time to study the picture, depending on when it was taken, they might be reminded of school life or a job, who their friends were, where they lived and who with.

You will need to encourage clients to allow themselves plenty of time to let their thoughts flow and to be selective and careful in choosing the memories to be represented within the home. Your role will be to support them as they become aware of how different pictures and memories make them feel, and encourage them to only stay with the ones that evoke positive emotions.

In practical terms there are various ways this footballing phase of your clients' lives can be incorporated into their homes. The traditional route would be to put one photograph of the time in a frame and display it in a prominent place. Alternatively, it could be enlarged to poster size then laminated or put into a clip frame and put on a wall. This more adventurous image is a bold and light-hearted reminder of their past.

Another way to bring this memory into your clients' homes is to use pictures of the actual place where they played. If they don't have any, then depending on where it was, you may be able to help them to go back and take some.

Even if they do have pictures of the place, going back to take some more might still be an excellent exercise to do. As individuals begin to open themselves up to the feelings and thoughts that will inevitably arise, the past will be brought into sharp focus alongside the present and they will begin to get some insight into how far they have actually come.

If your clients are fortunate enough to have a collection of photographs then they can create something a little more ambitious. By using a simple clip frame they can create a big impact with a collage of all their pictures, at varying times and places in their lives, cut and arranged just as they like them.

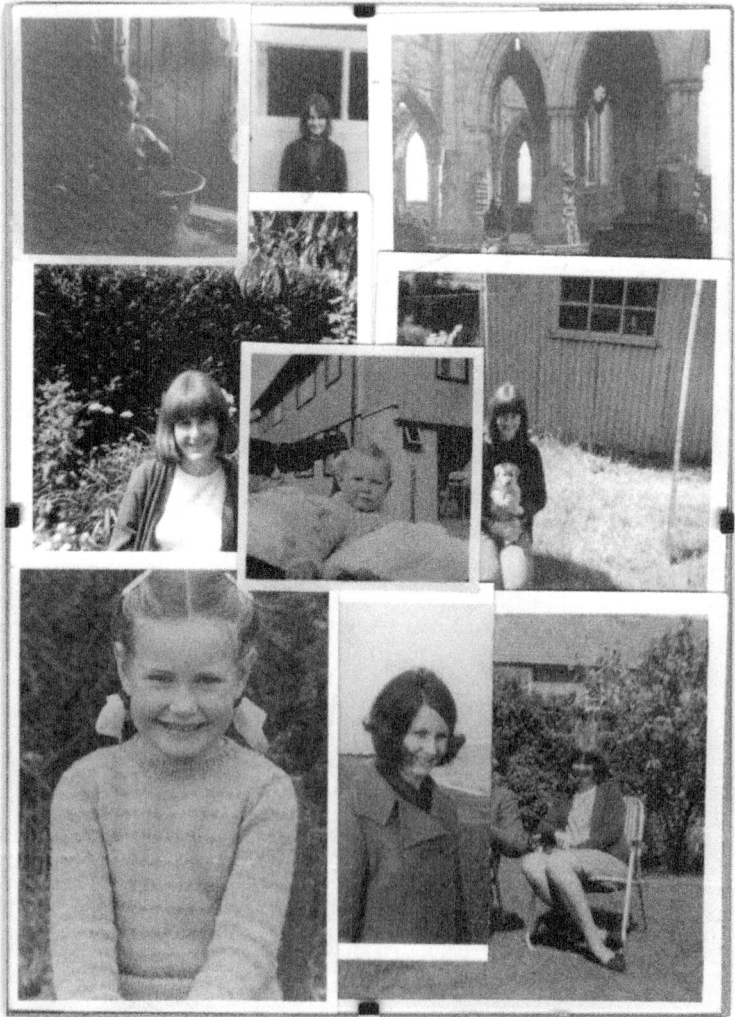

2.3 Significant People

Your clients' histories and identities will have been influenced by the people they have known. My book only focuses on the past in a positive way, and memories are only beneficial if they are brought into the present moment. Through memory, past events can be used to provide evidence of something that can help to give your clients a well-rounded view of the world and who they are. Memories of significant people can also provide a sort of yardstick which, when used reflectively, can show and encourage changes in patterns of their behaviour.

For example, individuals may recall becoming involved with people who they would have been better off without. This may have led to tension with the significant people in their lives at the time who would have been trying to have a positive influence. When looking back, they will be able to see and understand that a change has occurred in their thinking or behaviour. It doesn't matter if it is a lot or a little, they will be able to see that there has been some development and growth within themselves and that the significant people will have been influential in this, even if there is no longer contact with them.

Your clients will need time to think about who these important people in their lives might have been. As they come to mind, a list can be started, firstly of their names and then of everything that can be remembered about each of them. Individuals can then look at the list and consider which ones to represent in their home. There are no rules about how many, they can have lots or they can have one. This is a very personal decision, individuals will know how they feel.

Being involved in a good relationship with a significant person can provide motivation, confidence and a feeling of self-worth. If your clients can bring to mind positive memories of people who made them feel good, then it will be possible and beneficial to incorporate the feelings these memories evoke into their homes. This will provide a psychological boost which will help to broaden out and enrich their lives.

As you discuss this project with your clients, more and more of their memories will gradually start to come to the fore. You can use the list below to help you widen the conversation.

- Relationship to the person
- The person's age and gender
- At what period of life were they involved with the person?
- How old was the client at this time?
- How did they spend their time together?
- What was it about the person that the client liked or loved?
- Does the client still see them, would they want to?
- What did they talk about, did they laugh together?
- Did the person teach the client something significant?
- Did they have shared interests, what were they?

Aim to discuss all of these things with your clients to help them sort through their memories and feelings. When they are ready they can start to create something for the home which will bring these things together.

Project:

Personalised Picture

If there are photographs of the influential people in your clients' lives available, then these would be excellent to use. With a little thought and effort, a simple snapshot can be transformed into a unique item for the home. This will be a reminder of positive feelings from the past and one which will still have the power to make an individual feel good today.

To really bring to life their relationships in this way, your clients will need to identify the characteristics that will epitomise the people being remembered.

I have no way of knowing what aspects any of your clients would want to focus on so, for the sake of my book, I am going to illustrate this project by assuming that the person is being remembered for their ability to make a wonderful chocolate cake and that this is the first thing your clients think of when remembering being with them.

Illustrated below is my own memory of my grandmother, known to me as Nanna. She taught me how to embroider, in particular the stitches mentioned, how to make a stew and dumplings, and I have acknowledged that I felt loved whenever I was with her. I suggest you do this project yourself and, despite its simplicity, experience the real power of it.

Your clients will need to decide on a style of writing, a photograph and the type of card and frame to be used. If a photograph is not to hand and it's not possible to get one then maybe something related to that person can be used. For example, if he or she owned a cat then a photograph of a cat, similar to the one they owned, can be substituted, or maybe a garden if this is what they liked; it will not be difficult to find something relevant.

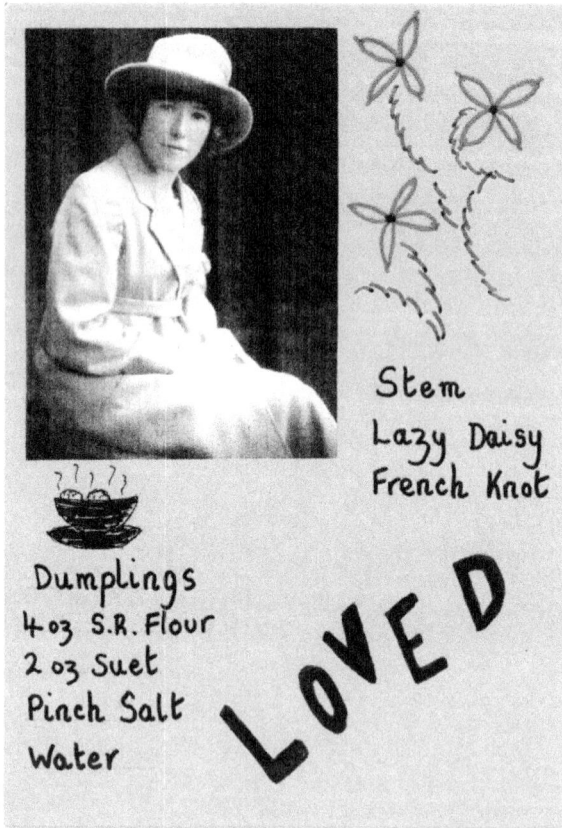

Stem
Lazy Daisy
French Knot

Dumplings
4 oz S.R. Flour
2 oz Suet
Pinch Salt
Water

LOVED

You will need to spend some time discussing with your clients the actual experience of what they share with their significant person. Using the chocolate cake for example, there would be the preparation, the doing, the smells and the feel of the whole event as well as the conversations that happened during these times. All this information can be used to represent the person in the drawing or writing.

How the person lived their life can be acknowledged by illustrating the card further, their hobbies and interests and anything known to be important to them can be included. For example, if they loved animals then the card could be illustrated with things to represent this. The whole of the mount can be covered with information about the person in the photograph as interpreted by your client.

During the time spent on this project, your clients will feel close to the individuals they are remembering, their minds will be full of the times they shared together and all sorts of snippets will filter back.

All of this will take time and sensitivity on your part but the finished item will be a tangible fusing together of your client's understanding of the relationship with the person represented and how he or she affected their life. It will be a combination of the personality of the remembered person and your client's very individual view of them. It will clearly show how this person is remembered and the time spent on the project presents the opportunity to revisit their relationship, not only bringing pleasure and pride but an amount of comfort too.

This whole process will help the people you work with recognise how these significant people may have influenced their lives. More than all of this, however, the finished projects will be a reminder that they have been cared for and valued, just for being themselves.

It really doesn't matter what the person is remembered for, it's not difficult to see that the example I have used can be swapped for almost anything, from stripping down a motorbike to going fishing, the technique will be the same. The important thing is that your clients are given the time and encouragement to understand and believe they are worthy of the care that has been shown.

The bringing together of the threads of your clients' lives within their homes is a significant task. Working through this project as well as using the finished item will go a long way towards providing a self-supporting environment. Through this work you will enable individuals to create a true sense of belonging within their accommodation.

Project:

Photograph – Place

Although this idea also uses photographs, it takes the concept of integrating the past into the present a little further. It uses pictures of a place where individuals spent time doing something they loved. If they haven't got any, depending on where it was, you might be able to help them to go back and take some. Going back to a significant place to take one or two up-to-date pictures is a good exercise but if this is not possible the project can be completed by using a good up-to-date photograph of themselves.

Going back to somewhere that holds fond memories can be risky. As we grow up we often internalise the influences of people who were involved in our upbringing and going back, even tentatively, to somewhere that will unlock memories may create overwhelming pressure and conflict within us.

The reality of the place might turn out to be very different to the cherished memory. Before working on this project your clients will need to be sure that they really are using a dependably good memory, and be aware of the risks. It's no good churning up negativity, a home requires positive influences. If they are not sure, ask them to write down the good and not so good things about it, and to be honest about any fears or worries they may have. They may decide that this is not a good memory after all and so won't use it, but if they decide that it is, they will also learn, by going over the pros and cons that even with good things there is often a mixture of emotions.

They should take time to choose just one photograph from the past and if possible, one taken recently of their chosen place where they enjoyed doing something they loved. Different sizes can be adjusted if necessary so that they can be framed side by side. Although this is a simple idea, it is an emotionally complex project. During the time your clients are working on it they will be reacquainting themselves with the person they used to be. By revisiting an area they once knew very well, either physically or just by memory, they will gradually come to understand and accept the transition that has happened between that time and now, allowing for greater awareness of how they evolved into the person they are now.

Your clients' histories are an integral part of who they are and only by being comfortable with it will they be able to establish themselves confidently in the present. By working towards achieving this they will prepare themselves for the challenges of independence and the outside world with a stronger sense of self.

This might be a demanding project for your clients, and could take a period of weeks or months to complete. However, the benefits it offers will be more than worth the effort and will serve to reinforce who they are on a daily basis.

2.4 Heroes

Still using the example of kicking a ball around as being the chosen memory, your clients will need to think about whether they had any footballing heroes at the time. If their interests were not football they may have had heroes of a different kind. If this was the case, they might still have old pictures or posters of people they admired, if not, with your help they could try to acquire some. Odds and ends like this can often be found by scouring boot sales and second-hand shops as well as online auction sites.

A simple and enjoyable way to display items like these would be to create a scrap book. Hard cover books with blank pages are cheap and easily available in supermarkets, or you can buy books specifically designed for the purpose. Everything your clients have that relate to their heroes can go in, they don't have to match or be in any particular order. Souvenirs like programmes and tickets as well as pictures can all be included. You can encourage individuals to be bold, they can decorate the scrap book in their own style and highlight the pieces that are particularly interesting to them.

Packaging items in a book like this is an excellent way to trace back and contain some of the positive threads of your clients' lives. The project will provide opportunities to unearth more and more of themselves and while these won't all be football related, what comes up will enable them to see a fuller picture of the time. This will help with easing their memories forward so that they can merge comfortably into the present and fit into their day-to-day lives without conflict.

The outcome of all this will be a creative and practical chunk of personal history. As well as providing a brilliant trip down memory lane, it will also be a great thing to share with friends who will no doubt have memories of their own to talk about.

If a client supported a particular team, either a local or a professional side, they may have something to represent them like a scarf or a hat. If this is the case, a hat can be hung up by the front door, a scarf can be draped around a picture. These are simple but strong reminders, every time they are seen, of good times.

If the team an individual supported still exists, is now the time to look them up again? You would need to help find out if they still play, how are they doing, is it possible to watch them again? Did your client have friends who supported them too? Where are they now and would it be appropriate to make contact?

Football team colours can be used within a home to show allegiance to a side. These colours are often bold and bright, red for example represents courage, vigour and strength so is ideal in the context of sport. Colours generally can be used as huge statements about who we are and they have a language of their own. However, colours such as this can have a very unsettling effect or create a feeling of unease so it would be sensible for your clients to use them sparingly.

More subtle ways to introduce this memory through colour would be to buy crockery, bedlinen, cushions and towels in various shades of the team colours. These don't all have to match, a mixture of shades and shapes will provide the opportunity to display individuality and taste. They don't have to be expensive either, charity shops and inexpensive houseware shops and supermarkets are all quite affordable. The trick is for your clients to stay focused, if they want to use a colour to represent who they are or what their interests are they must only buy those items that will speak of this.

The basic concept of using colour can have a huge impact on the way your clients feel about their homes. They will have a connection with it and the efforts made will be an everyday reminder of the spirit of the time it represents and the pleasure they got from it.

I have used football as the chosen memory but the techniques for introducing this into your clients' homes are the same whatever the memory might be.

2.5 Music

Another very powerful way to evoke memories is through music. Even if your clients think they were not taking much notice of this in the past, the chances are that whatever was popular at the time would have been playing like a backdrop to their lives and they would have been subconsciously listening.

Music, however, can be like photographs. It has the potential to unlock all sorts of feelings and emotions. If the last time your clients heard a piece of music was at a significant time in their lives then they will need to prepare themselves for the possible impact they might feel when they hear it again.

You can help individuals to identify what was popular at any given time by doing a simple search online. Boot sales, charity shops and online auctions are a brilliant way to pick up old CDs; this powerful medium will jog the memory and bring all sorts of reminiscences flooding back.

Music is an excellent way to bring the past alive within a home. Favourite pieces from a particular era can be used to lift spirits. Hopefully the people you work with will learn to put it on when they are doing mundane chores, just to relieve the monotony and to make themselves smile.

Finally, if kicking a ball around really was a good memory for your clients then they need to get a ball and do it again, just for the fun of it.

It is not difficult to see that it is possible for individuals not only to express themselves by using a simple memory, but the experience can be used as a tool for beginning to understand and accept the past. The concept of the ball can easily be swapped with other everyday activities, it doesn't have to be complicated and neither does the way it is used within the home.

Remember there are no limits to the number of memories used, the more creative a client can be, the more personal their home will feel and the greater the connection and sense of satisfaction they will experience.

An individual's cultural journey is important and their home is where it can be displayed with confidence and freedom. Remember that as memories come into consciousness, so will emotions, your work needs to be sensitive and slow and you must allow each person the time they need to consider things calmly.

2.6 Traditions and Rituals

The chances are your clients will not have had a stereotypical childhood and their cultural identities will be the result of the many different circumstances and people who have influenced them. This fact will serve to reinforce just how individual they are, but could also create inner conflict as they struggle to get a balance between their individuality and the need to be just like everybody else.

This is another area where individuals may need lots of time to think when it comes to considering just how they can represent themselves within their homes. With regard to traditions and rituals, they are the only ones to know what they need to hold on to from their pasts and what would be best left behind.

Maybe without realising it, all the people you work with will have some inbuilt traditions and rituals coming from the lives they have known. These may have been thought about carefully and created with purpose, or they may have been handed down over the years without much thought. For example, a roast dinner on a Sunday is carried on by most people simply because it is what they were brought up with, but this provides them with the precious foundation for emotional bonding with people they love, all sharing in the meal and the history of the tradition.

Whatever they might be and however they come about, rituals and traditions within the context of home are something that can create security, provide structure for day-to-day living, bring about feelings of happiness and a true sense of belonging. They will be incredibly important in your clients' homes because they can also strengthen a shaky sense of self and promote feelings of well-being.

Some everyday rituals we take for granted, we don't think too much about why we do them or what they have to offer but very often they underpin our cultural identity as well as our relationships and lives. For example, funerals can help with easing raw emotions to a place of healing while celebrations can help with transition, maybe to a new home or job.

Rituals come in all sorts of guises and below is a selection of what an average family might have in place.

Sunday roast

Walk at the weekend

Takeaway meal on a designated evening

Exercise routine

Walk the dog after tea

Cake with candles on birthday

Meal out on anniversary

One evening a week with nothing to do

Individually some of these traditions may seem insignificant but, for your clients, creating a sense of belonging in their homes is crucial and it will be these everyday things, carried on with regularity that will establish their lives and who they are. By putting some of these in place themselves they can provide psychological structure and a feeling of safety at a time when they may feel most vulnerable.

Once an individual has got used to their chosen traditions or rituals it can be surprising what an impact they will feel if these are then taken away. On a personal level I experienced missing out on one of my own rituals recently when I had some building work done within my home. For around two weeks the dining room was out of use. This meant we ate on trays, often while watching television, and I kept things simple by using condiments and picking up cutlery in the kitchen. When the meal was over there was no hanging about, it didn't take a minute to clear away and wash up. Although this was not a problem in itself, and the meal was the same, I found I missed the time I usually spent laying the table, and the general feeling of anticipation. I also missed the familiarity and comfort of sitting at the table and allowing conversation to happen naturally. During this short time, meal times were really only about the business of eating food.

I soon understood that, without realising it, I had got used to this meal being more than just eating, it was a time for catching up on the day, for myself it provided the opportunity to think or talk, it truly had become a ritual.

With this in mind, when your clients move on, many of their known traditions and rituals will be gone from their lives and, like me, they may well not be aware of just what they will miss when they eventually move. Your job therefore is to help each person identify those that are happening now so they can consider which ones are important enough to keep.

Below is a list of events that use rituals and traditions. Use it to help get you started in conversations with your clients to explore how they feel about them and what rituals they have known around them in the past. For example, 'food' might trigger memories of certain meals being prepared for regular visitors, significant meals during the week or just a favourite meal they used to enjoy on a regular basis.

Religion, Christmas festivities or other

Birthdays, their own or other peoples

Language written and spoken

Food

Leisure activities

Music and dance

Art

Clothes

Previous homes

School

Simple traditions, like watching a favourite television programme, can contribute greatly to a sense of identity and clients will need to think about what they would want to continue to do, not only for themselves but also for other people. For example, on birthdays or at Christmas they may well enjoy receiving cards or presents but they might also really enjoy giving them. With a little forethought and organisation something like this can be continued after independence. By carrying on with simple things such as this, an individual is not only living out their personal values but also bringing aspects of their past smoothly into the present.

You can help your clients to consider everything on the list and encourage them to think through the way they have experienced them. There may well be some traditions they have known that they will not want in their new homes, but some may have special significance in representing who they are. These are the ones to hold on to.

To jog the memory further you can help clients to separate memories into categories, Traditions, Celebrations and Rituals.

Traditions are the things that are handed down pretty much without question from one generation to another, like the Sunday roast.

Celebrations are the things we do for birthdays, religious festivals like Christmas and anniversaries or achievements.

Rituals are repeated actions of any kind and these can be created without needing history to validate them.

There are many types of traditions and rituals. For example, some are designed to involve more than one person, like a wedding or an annual community fireworks display, while others may be quite solitary, but no less meaningful for the person involved. Some may be family centred and may be very specific to the family carrying them out, like saying grace or having specific bedtime rituals with children, and some will be culture centred, like Diwali, the Hindu festival of light, and will carry a much broader meaning.

Moving to independent living is a major life event and will involve changes in relationships and lifestyle. These things in themselves will bring about a change in your clients. So, if they are to go through this transition successfully they will need to recognise that some of their known traditions or rituals may need to be modified a little in order to accommodate new circumstances, feelings and emotions after moving.

All traditions and rituals need to be kept simple and fun. If things are too complicated or expensive they just won't work. For example, your clients may be looking forward to resuming or continuing the luxury of enjoying a meal in a restaurant once a month; after independence, this idea can be kept alive by modifying it. Getting a simple takeaway or inviting a friend round to share the meal will soon turn into a sustainable event.

It is affordable, fairly easy to arrange and therefore achievable, thus providing an amount of continuity and emotional security.

Your clients will need to be cautious about which of their known traditions they bring into their new homes. They will need to be sure they are not trying to hold on to the past because they don't want to face the future. The traditions they recreate really do need to be about them and their independence. Used appropriately, the experiences they will be drawing on are all part of who they are and by bringing them into their homes in a positive way they are recognising personal history and creating a sense of belonging.

Once your clients have worked out the traditions they would like to carry forward they can then start to think about establishing some new ones of their own.

For these to be a success, they will need to come from the heart. Rituals, however small and simple, can be powerful tools that can add significant value to the way your clients see life in their new accommodation, they therefore need to be genuinely about themselves. It usually takes between three to six weeks for a new practice to start to feel familiar so each one will need to be given time and practised regularly if it's going to have a fair chance of survival. However, your clients will gradually see that by perseverance and staying focused, some pleasure in it will soon begin to emerge, they will begin to look forward to the experience as well as the improved sense of security and well-being that each one will bring.

Before moving to independent living is the right time for this work and you can help your clients to begin to put one or two new traditions in place that they will be able to carry through to their new lives.

For example, if at the end of the day your clients generally feel tired or bored, they can create an 'end of the day' ritual. This can involve allowing themselves to do nothing for half an hour after getting in or at a set time, except sit and watch television with a treat to eat. Once a ritual like this has become established, this time of the day will be something to look forward to.

Below are a few very simple suggestions of other new traditions to help get ideas flowing.

Keep a journal

Music, listen to or play

Grooming, hair, makeup, teeth

Keep 'to do' list

Recognise all the seasons as well as significant days such as Mayday, summer and winter solstice

Exercise

Make a positive phone call once a week

It is very easy for any of us to develop negative rituals. If your clients have done this, you can help with identifying what they are and then providing guidance towards an understanding of why it is not a good idea to continue with them. This is something that many individuals may find incredibly difficult and therefore they will probably resist any change. Patience and sensitivity on your part is crucial.

Any ritual or tradition can be considered to be not good if it leaves the person performing it feeling unsettled in any way. The reason that traditions and rituals have benefits is that they are positive acts, if this is not the case then they need to be stopped. If any habit, ritual or tradition leaves your clients feeling emotionally vulnerable, confused, or it doesn't have an appropriate beginning or end, then they are best not to be carried on. Your clients may well need your help with changing habits and switching the negative acts for positive ones.

Rituals can be incredibly varied and created around very practical things. Some may be daily like showering and dressing at a certain time, some weekly like buying a favourite magazine, and some less frequent than that. For example, if your clients have a lot of work to get through on a regular basis, they can create a simple ritual for when this is achieved. This might be something like playing a favourite computer game or lying in a scented bath.

There is a subtle difference between a routine and a ritual. A routine is generally something that is done just for the sake of doing it with little thought or feeling, like emptying the bins. A ritual will be something that has some meaning for the participant and will therefore be done with thought, feeling and some pleasure.

All traditions and rituals consist of three stages, the Preparation, the Experiencing and then the Phasing Out. Although these different stages are subtle, they are all interlinked and important, together they make the most of the experience.

If for example, the tradition is a Friday night tea from the local fish and chip shop then the preparation would include the recognition of the time, getting ready to go out, the trip to the shop, laying the table or tray, putting the food on the plate and sitting down with it.

By the time this has all been done it's time for the actual tradition itself. This is the Experiencing stage. With the fish and chip tradition it will be the actual eating of the food and interacting with anybody else who is sharing the meal. This can also be done while watching a television programme, listening to music or in silence.

Next there is the Phasing Out stage, this is when you begin to tidy things away and begin to let go of the experience both physically and from your mind. This stage is incredibly important with regard to structure. If the meal is not tidied away properly and plates are left on the table or condiments not put away, the whole thing will become undefined and will lose some meaning. All traditions and rituals need a beginning, a middle and a positive and appropriate ending.

A simple ritual like this one will bring some context to the working week; psychologically your clients will know that it's Friday, the weekend is here and the evening will have a different feel to it. It will also bring about a feeling of security because it is part of a known and trusted structure. When the ritual becomes established it increases in status because it will then have memory and history too, these things create a sense of belonging and warmth, which will add substantial emotional value to the home where it is carried out. Besides all of this there is the pleasure of eating the meal!

These small actions must never be underestimated, and what starts out as a simple ritual adding some structure to the week, if it's kept up, will eventually evolve into a long-term tradition that may well be passed on to other people in your clients' lives.

I have used the fish and chip scenario because I have no way of knowing what type of ritual your clients may want to create, but when they have some ideas on what they need then you will be able to help them to think through some of the practicalities involved.

Below are some of the things your clients will need to think about before starting any new ritual.

When it will happen?

What is needed?

Will there always be the time?

Is concentration possible?

Is anybody else involved?

What about interruptions?

If you are able to help your clients prepare themselves for independence by getting some traditions and rituals in place before they move it will help enormously with the whole procedure. Having this structure to their lives will affirm an individual's identity and create a strong sense of belonging in their new accommodation.

2.7 Food

Project:

Food Memory Journal

The use of food is a powerful tool in the defining of an identity and as you work through my book with your clients they can learn to use it to their advantage. By using their own food history they can create a real sense of belonging within their homes and learn to protect themselves from using food in a negative or harmful way. A negative approach to food is often fuelled by the desire to be accepted and recognised. By using their personal connections with food positively an individual will gradually build up confidence and develop a stronger sense of self.

The very basics your clients will need in relation to food are set out below, but take time to have discussions with them about this, they may well come up with a few different items that they see as essential.

Table or tray

Cutlery

Cup and glass

Plate, dish

Saucepans

Mixing bowls

Chopping board

Place mat to absorb heat

Dish for cooking in oven or microwave

Use of fridge

Many of these items can be picked up cheaply at supermarkets, charity shops or boot sales and can be collected gradually. If they can be acquired before the move it will help to focus a client's mind on the reality of their situation and prevent an attitude of denial about what the future really holds.

When it happens, the move to independence may feel completely overwhelming for your clients and preparing meals may be the last thing on their minds. In order to stay healthy and out of debt some coping strategies for this time will need to be about food and what their concepts of this might be.

Food is a multi-layered subject and can be used for much more than nutrition. Your clients will have had some sort of relationship with it since the day they were born and this will have affected many aspects of their lives, including how they see themselves, not only as individuals, but also in relation to other people and the wider society.

The time and money an individual spends on choosing and preparing food for themselves will be a strong indicator about how they see themselves. Laying a place setting for example, only takes a couple of minutes but if they are feeling worthless they will not bother with it, they will eat when they're hungry and not be too fussy or spend much time thinking about it.

When a client can discover and acknowledge their personal history with food they will be able to develop awareness to what it means to them now in various contexts.

They are then able to use food within their home in a way which will endorse their cultural history as well as bring about a sense of belonging within the home.

Some of the ways, other than nutrition, that food can be used are listed below.

Social activity

Control

Reward

Exclusion

Comfort

Leveller

Creativity

Making a statement

So that your clients can begin to consider food within the context of their homes, all of these ways of using it should gradually be discussed. They will need to draw on past experiences such as places and people they have known and try to recognise how these experiences affect what they are comfortable with today and what, if anything, might need to be changed for the future.

During 2010 the University of California carried out a study for the Institute of European Studies on Food, Culture and Identity and they came up with the concept that food may be used "as a way of promoting Tolerance and Diversity".[5] This may seem a long way from the clients you are working with but it shows the power of food and how it

---

[5] *Food, Culture and Identity in a Global Context*: Institute of European Studies at University of California, p.3, Internet Article

can be used as an inclusive or an exclusive tool. For example, any of us may have been taken to a restaurant whose menus were written in a foreign language, such as French or Italian. Unless we could speak those languages this might have made us feel like outsiders who are not included in the specialist nature of the food.

On the opposite end of the spectrum we may have shared a meal in an informal and welcoming environment where the food acted as a great leveller, as a means to bond and break down barriers and where status or knowledge were unimportant. Your clients will need to identify any experiences of this nature and whilst they may not have been as extreme as this, the outcomes would have been the same. Individuals can then consider how these experiences fit with who they are today. For example, using these examples, they could ask themselves if they would want to learn the language that might have intimidated them in the restaurant so that they could walk into a similar restaurant feeling confident and equal to everyone else there or, would they prefer to opt out of a culture of this nature and just let it go.

By thinking through scenarios that they have known, and considering how they feel about them now, individuals can help themselves to create a relationship with food that will provide an identity they have control over and one which will only change when they decide they want it to.

Use the list below to jog the memory and discuss how food has been experienced.

Parties/celebrations

Occasion cakes

Sunday breakfast

Tea and cake

When friends drop in

Illness

Bedtime drinks

Endings

Cultural celebrations

Days out

Special treats

The way your clients have seen food forms part of their cultural heritage and identity but they may well have known many people who had very different ways of using it. For example, although English, Caribbean, and Asian families may all celebrate the same occasion, it could be a very different experience in each of their homes. Your clients may have known many different forms of eating and consequently, now feel confused about their cultural background. They may have the feeling that they are not quite whole in some way, that they don't have enough of any culture to really belong. Your work will help clients to acknowledge that their history is valid and by raising their awareness of how they feel about it they will really understand and value who they are.

Through this work you can encourage individuals to look at food from a broader perspective, discuss with them what they would consider to be most important, the cost of their food or the way it is farmed. For example, organic and free range are more expensive, would they prefer to eat more at a cheaper price or less and have better quality? Discuss whether they agree with eating meat and whether they have an opinion on how animals are treated. You can then introduce a discussion around how they feel about large supermarket chains – would they want to support a local independent store and if so, why?

How people feel about these issues influences things like budget, the food they prepare, what they read or watch on television and their diet.

Your clients can record their thoughts on all these subjects in a Food Memory Journal which you can help them to create.

A Food Memory Journal needs to be a substantial notebook, preferably with a hard cover so that it lasts. These are easily available at most supermarkets and can be decorated or covered to make it personal. The words 'Food Memory Journal' need to be written clearly on the front so the book is not used for anything else.

It is important that this Journal is not confused with a recipe or cookbook. The Food Memory Journal will be a very personal link to connections with food and crucial in the understanding of the past. It can be used whenever something of importance is remembered connected with food. It can also be used to set goals, maybe to track down a particular ingredient or to visit somebody who made wonderful dinners or record the best meals and why they were so good. There doesn't have to be time limits, it is the remembering that is so important and this in itself will help a client to recognise that during the past they have been cared for and happy.

When individuals you are working with identify what they really feel connected to and what is genuinely part of the complicated mix that they are today, they can begin to fill in some of the gaps they might feel around their identity. By introducing some of these food-related issues into their lives on a regular basis they will bring real and meaningful connections with the past right into the present. This in itself will provide a strong chance of success in independent living.

Below are some questions to prompt discussion and thought about approaches to eating. When a client is living by themselves they will be able to do anything they like around food; discussions like these will encourage questioning not only why they may be doing some things but also whether some practices are really good for them.

121

Do you like to eat at set times?

Do you get up as soon as you have finished eating?

Do you watch television while eating?

Do you speak on the phone during mealtimes?

Do you walk around while eating?

Do you snack a lot during the day and then don't need a 'proper' meal?

Do you sit at a table?

Are you more comfortable with other people or alone?

Do you enjoy food?

Are you open to trying new foods?

Do you like large/small portions?

When these things are talked about with your clients you need to allow plenty of time for them to really think through their answers. They may be surprised at how they really feel about some of them and will need gentle support from you to help them gradually understand their emotions. For example, an individual may feel very strongly that they need to watch a particular television programme every week while eating tea on their lap. This might simply be because they have memories of doing this with someone they loved.

However, they may also feel that the time is coming to make a change and might be considering letting a routine like this go. Although to an outsider this might appear to be a relatively simple change, it could carry with it all kinds of implications and may fill a client with feelings of guilt, anger and sadness.

Working on a complex subject like this will need a lot of patience and gentleness on your part and there will be all sorts of valid reasons why clients may or may not want to carry forward some of the things they have known in the past. Listening to them and showing that you are there to support and encourage is your job; given time, individuals will begin to develop real belief in themselves.

A good way to create opportunities for discussion is to spend time working together informally in a kitchen. Here you will be able to talk generally about likes and dislikes and casually bring in many of the issues above.

As confidence around food and in the kitchen grows you can encourage clients to cook for other people so they can experience some of the rewards that this activity brings. Working through recipes improves all sorts of skills from time management to patience. Gradually, and with your encouragement, all the stages from preparation, cooking, presentation and serving can be covered.

Sharing a meal we have prepared ourselves with another person increases the pressure to make it a success, but the rewards are all the richer. The whole exercise focuses the mind and provides an enormous sense of achievement as well as fantastic meals.

Your clients may surprise themselves and discover they have an artistic streak, or find that they enjoy breaking lots of recipe rules. These things allow individuals to have total control over what and how they cook and as they get used to handling and experiencing food successfully, self-esteem and confidence will continue to grow. They will develop some basic skills that will be invaluable in their homes as well as making them very popular individuals!

During the time you have working with your clients and as their interest in this subject increases, you can encourage them to think about creating their own signature dish.

A signature dish is one that can be used for lots of different occasions, one that people recognise as being made by a particular individual and one that speaks about this individual in some way. As individuals make their signature dish more and more times it will become second nature and they will enjoy preparing and sharing it as well as using it as a contribution, a gift or a friendly gesture.

Your clients will all need to make their own decisions about what this dish might be. It could be something they would like to develop from previous knowledge and experience or it might be something completely new that reflects the impending status of independence. You can encourage individuals to be brave and free with their ideas and remind them there are no rules. If they want to, they can use their genealogy to influence their creations, using a traditional recipe and then tweaking it to make it all their own.

Your clients' signature dishes can be literally any type of food they want to prepare. It can be cooked or uncooked, hot or cold, savoury or sweet. They can create a sauce, either sweet or savoury, a marinade, a preserve, a cake or biscuits or it can be kept really simple and adopt biscuits and cheese simply by using their favourites and arranging them in their own special signature way. Anything that sparks their imaginations can be written down in their Food Memory Journal.

2.8 Personal Kitchen

Project:

Food Mood Board

During the build-up to independence your clients can begin to collect appropriate items to have in their cooking spaces which can go beyond the bare essentials. The reality of this space is that it might be a small corner of a multi-purpose room or it might be a designated space which has to be shared with other people. The important point here is that whatever the space is like, it is still possible for individuals to put their mark on it.

You will have the opportunity to talk to your clients about items which hold significance for them from kitchens they have previously known and these can be noted in the Food Memory Journal. Their cooking spaces will probably be made up of pieces collected from a variety of sources, possibly some of the original items from people they used to know or live with. It is likely though that the majority will come from boot sales, charity shops and supermarkets.

Individuals need to be guided by their feelings about items they have around them and also remember that the only design rules in their homes are the ones they make for themselves.

It is very important that the cooking area is conducive to reflection and constructive thinking so that when an individual is working in it their thoughts and feelings can flow easily. Having familiar objects around will enhance the link to the past and this space, however large or small, busy or quiet, may well evolve into the place where they have their most creative thoughts and make some sound decisions.

As a way of bringing food alive within the home a food mood board can be created by using an inexpensive cork board. If a client goes out somewhere special to eat they can bring back a small souvenir like a business card or promotional leaflet and pin it to the board. They can also look for food-related articles that interest them and pictures that represent places they would like to visit. This may spark an interest in different food cultures leading to experimenting with new recipes. The board can also be used to put up other people's recipes that have been enjoyed and anything they would like to try out. This whole mixture will provide a powerful source of ideas and inspiration that can be seen every day.

Food is an essential and complex component of your clients' daily lives. By recognising the past through the way they deal with it in their new homes they will gradually build confidence and a sense of belonging. They will also develop the ability to promote and enjoy social occasions as well as having an insight into maintaining their health and their budget.

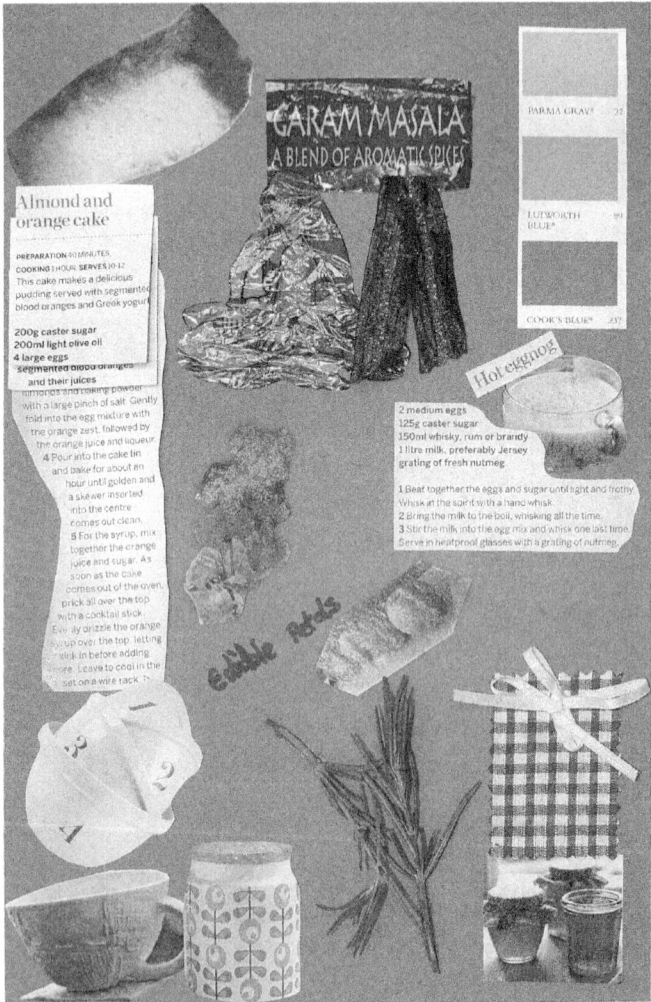

2.9 Belief Systems

My book covers many issues to provide practical help towards the well-being of the people you work with as they move towards independence. However, besides their cultural and biographical histories there is another dimension to each individual that can also colour and influence their life in a dramatic way.

Since ancient times humans have looked towards a higher being or force and have aspired to understanding the universe and where we fit within it. Today, we can still look at and walk around age-old sacred sites and can only wonder what the philosophy behind them was about. Because we remain curious about these things, theories abound and the sustaining feature of us as human beings is that this depth of wonderment does not leave us.

Your clients will be no exception and will have this depth within themselves; it might be hidden, blocked, or denied. However, to give them the best chance of succeeding in independence you will need to help them explore their thoughts and feelings around the subject of a belief system.

Because you will be adopting a whole-person approach in your work, spiritual well-being will be regarded as important as emotional and mental health. All of these things are very closely connected and balanced within each individual and if your clients have not yet considered their spirituality in any way, they will be at a great disadvantage at the very time when they will need all the self-reliance they can muster.

Being in touch with our spirituality is something we all experience from time to time in our lives, even though we may not recognise it or label it as such. These experiences can be anything from feeling indefinably moved while watching something natural like a sunset, to taking time out in a sacred place.

How it manifests itself will differ from person to person but your work on this topic, through my book, will provide your clients with the opportunity to think things through slowly, enabling them to take an objective view of what their possible beliefs could ultimately be.

According to the Dalai Lama[6] you do not have to have a belief system to be a spiritual person. He speaks of two kinds of spirituality, one is where a religious belief has been identified and is practised with conviction and the second is one that he believes all of mankind can strive towards, whether he has an identified belief or not.

This second type he calls "basic spirituality" and describes it as being the qualities of goodness, kindness, compassion and caring. Whatever our beliefs, or even if we have none, if we live with these qualities in mind they will naturally lead us to a higher level of thinking and behaving, and therefore increase the chances of us enjoying a more spiritual existence.

For me, although I have a belief system in place, on a day-to-day basis spirituality is about having some kind of connection with the universe around me. I find it comforting to think that every one of us comes from the same source. I try hard, although it can be difficult at times, to always look for the light shining in another person. I have learnt that pain and difficult circumstances usually bring about growth and understanding. I also believe that spirituality is not all one way; as individuals we can show ourselves the respect and love that we would show to somebody else and seek the light in ourselves that is so often dimmed through the ups and downs of our lives.

It is possible that your clients may already be in touch with their spirituality one way or another. Many people become very inquisitive and interested in all sorts of routes that might take them on to a higher path. Whether it be conventional or

---

[6] *The Art of Happiness*, p.258, HH Dalai Lama & Howard Cutler

something completely alternative, if an individual is involved with a genuine, spiritual community it could be a potential resource that could provide them with security and companionship.

Belonging to a group of people who share the same belief or faith can bring comfort and support to your clients that would otherwise not be there. As well as this, the depth of their spiritual thinking is acknowledged; this kind of like-mindedness affirms who they are and helps to build confidence in their own judgement. When their awareness of themselves as spiritual beings slips into place within their psyche, then everything around them will feel more comfortable.

Clearly we are three dimensional beings and Virginia Satir[7] says that spirituality can be discussed openly within a non-religious context. With my book in mind, it is part of your work with your clients to broach this subject in a way which will be unbiased and nonspecific. Below are some discussion points for you to use to promote thinking in your clients when the time is right.

- Did you attend church or other religious instruction as a child?

- Do you ever wonder what happens when you die?

- How do you think the world was created?

- Have you been Christened or gone through another religious ceremony? What does this mean to you now?

- What do you feel when you see natural phenomena, perhaps a rainbow or a storm?

- Do you ever pray?

---

[7] *The New People Making*, p.334-341, Virginia Satir

- Does kindness or caring motivate you?

By encouraging your clients to take a whole-person approach to their own lives, thereby recognising their spirituality, research has shown[8] that depression is less likely to occur and, as confidence grows with further explorations into the subject, feelings of self-worth will naturally increase.

Below are some practical ideas to help you to take your work with your clients a little deeper.

- Take notice of what is really being said during conversations on the subject.

- Share time with individuals looking at things that might promote a sense of wonder —these can include any place or building with spiritual meaning, a church, a stone circle, woodland, the sea, the night sky, a new baby, clouds, natural lake or stream, artwork.

- Reading, tune in to what your clients are telling you about their thoughts and feelings and try to obtain material to promote or expand their convictions or theories. Try not to be shy about challenging a negative attitude at times.

Generally speaking, if we can have awareness to our spiritual selves then we can start to look beyond the mundane everyday stuff that we all get bogged down in. It helps us to look towards real meaning, harmony and peace, both within ourselves and in our immediate environment. Anything that can help keep your clients' minds focused on positive aspects

---

[8] *Understanding Youth: Perspectives, Identities and Practices*, p.205, Ed. Mary Jane Kehily

of life will prove an invaluable tool in helping them achieve sustained success.

CONCEPT THREE

ALLOW YOUR HOME TO INSPIRE AND NURTURE YOU – IT IS YOUR PLACE FOR CREATIVITY AND FREEDOM OF THOUGHT

---

*"The symptom of uncreative living is the feeling that
nothing means anything, of futility, I couldn't care less."*
D. W. Winnicott

This third Concept has been placed at the end of the book to illustrate that most of us need to have the basics to our lives in place before we can focus on the more imaginative and creative side to our natures. When we are able to feel relaxed and reasonably safe, ideas and inspiration usually flow much more freely.

Through Concepts One and Two your clients will have thought a lot about the foundations and safety of their lives and homes as well as their personal histories, bringing an awareness of how this features in where they are right now. It is inevitable that the natural thought processes and emotions attached to these issues will take time to evolve but the outcome of this will eventually strengthen and underpin their lives in a new home environment.

You are in the fortunate position of having opportunities

to explore another dimension to life with your clients – their creativity. You will be able to dispel the myth that creativity is an expensive luxury; within the context of home, it need not be. Individuals can begin to experiment and experience the sense of empowerment that using this side of their nature will bring, even when carrying out the most mundane chores.

To begin with, individuals may find it strange to experience the freedom of expression that living alone can bring, and it may not come easily. They may find that allowing themselves to really explore their thoughts and ideas to any depth is quite difficult because they are not used to it. This might be the first time that some of your clients have really taken this side of themselves seriously.

Through the work you do individuals will begin to understand the value and worth of what their imagination holds. Although my book suggests traditional methods of creativity, there really are no boundaries and clients might surprise themselves with their originality. They may start to get creative around anything from packed lunches to cleaning the bathroom, all helping to keep lethargy at bay. Immense confidence can be gained through a home and the people you work with will learn how to allow their environment to nurture that very sensitive, and complex part of themselves that is so unique, their imaginative self.

Acquiring freedom of thought can be like acquiring any new skill. We all get into habits with our thinking and can get into set thought patterns which are repetitive and restricting, putting in unnecessary boundaries and limiting our abilities. It might be difficult for your clients to break old habits and begin to allow their thoughts and ideas to be free, it might also be quite challenging for them to take them seriously and really believe they are valid and worthy of respect.

Creativity is something that can't be used up; the more it is used, the more it will flow. Adding this extra dimension to life and home will contribute dramatically to your clients' physical and mental well-being. They may be genuinely surprised at what ideas they have and how much confidence they gain by merely knowing that these ideas have come from nowhere but inside themselves.

3.1 Overcoming Boredom

Inevitably there will be obstacles along the way, below is a list of the more common ones that can stop artistic or creative ideas from flowing.

Concerns or worries about finance

Lack of daily structure or routine

A sense of feeling out of control

Boredom

Having no real focus or goals to work towards, drifting

Clearly there are many potential hurdles to overcome but the main thing that will prevent your clients from getting in touch with their inspirational side will be boredom. Boredom is the enemy of creativity and is an emotional state that can creep up on any of us. Boredom, if not held in check, can gradually lead to lack of motivation and depression.

Dr Lars Svendsen[9] states that there are two types of boredom. One type is 'situational' where a person is in a position of waiting, perhaps for a bus or a doctor's appointment. The other type is 'repetitive' where a person has to keep repeating the same action. Your clients may be vulnerable to

---

[9] *A Philosophy of Boredom*, Dr Lars Svendsen, Internet Article

both of these types of boredom, finding themselves with gaps in time that they haven't yet learnt how to fill appropriately, and having things to do that are mundane and repetitive. If boredom is not recognised and kept in check it can lead to low moods and lack of motivation as it gets a grip.

Anything creative should be stimulating and fun, there are no boundaries and as your clients become more confident their imagination will really begin to fly. Below are some ideas you can use to introduce to your clients to aid the unlocking of their imaginations.

Writing and drawing

Dancing

Clothing, designing and making

Being a child again

Reducing stress and anxiety

Provide precious space or thinking time

Music, listening to or playing

Exercise and sport

Doing something nice for somebody

Be in touch with other creative people

All of these things can be used by all of us to open our minds, and the people you work with are no exception. Encourage them to try a few off the list, some will have more impact than others. You will be able to identify what is right for individuals by picking up on their comments or ideas, when this happens you can then work with them to really begin to bring out their creative side.

Without realising it your clients may already be expressing themselves artistically and it might show in any of these ways:

Clothing

Hairstyles

Reading material

Music

Dancing

Any activities or special interests

What is valued and kept within own living space

If you take notice of all of these things you will be able to tune into how a client's creativity is coming out already, you can then build on this to encourage trying something new. These things should be fun, enjoy them together!

3.2 Be a Child

Preparing for independent living can be stressful and worrying. It can be a relief and a luxury to sometimes allow ourselves to revert back to childhood. Doing something we used to enjoy as a child is not reserved for young people; whatever age we are, this is a guilt-free way to indulge ourselves in things we can still get pleasure from.

Being a child every now and then would provide a positive balance to your clients' lives. Allowing themselves to switch from the seriousness of their situations into something much more free and funny will create opportunities to laugh, relax and keep things in perspective.

You can reassure individuals that silliness is alright sometimes, everybody needs to feel that life is still fun.

Each of us will have different memories of having fun and

you might find that when you think about your own they make you squirm with embarrassment. Alternatively, they might fill you with a warm joy as you remember what it was like to have nothing more to worry about than how to build an indoor tent. Encouraging your clients to experiment a little with this idea is a must, there are various ways shown below to help get things moving.

Learn to tell jokes

Play games, alone or with friends

Make friends with people who bring on a smile

Eat favourite childhood food

Buy favourite childhood sweets

Get outside, fly a kite, kick a ball, skateboard, roller skate

Watch favourite childhood DVD

Get on a trampoline

Play Twister

Go fishing

Eventually your clients will be able to use their homes as the base from which these ideas will grow and through this they can show how they spend their 'child time'. A skateboard can be propped up where it can be seen every day, creating an air of anticipation. Games can also be left in a place where they can be seen.

You are in a position to show that letting go of their grown-up sides for a while can become an integral part of their lives and their homes are where they can enjoy the afterglow of this type of activity.

3.3 Self Nurturing

After moving to independence there will undoubtedly be times when your clients will feel very alone and possibly frightened. It could be a trying time as they begin to fully understand the way their lives have evolved and the consequences of this. Individuals may have lost contact with people they love or be finding it hard to find work. Whatever their difficulties, they need to recognise that home, wherever it is, will always be the one place where they can feel nurtured and cared for and the probability is that they will be the provider of these things themselves.

Your clients need to be able to recognise feelings that can bring them down or make them feel low and then spend some time discovering how they can help themselves. By being prepared, individuals will have a much greater chance of keeping negative emotions at bay and preventing a descent into loss of confidence and motivation which could so easily sabotage their chances of making a success of their new lives.

Working through my book will help individuals to recognise what works well for them and enable them to get into the habit of recognising and dealing with these feelings as soon as they arise. The suggestions below will help you to encourage clients to try something different and to be aware of how this makes them feel.

- Do something you really enjoy but much slower than usual
- Learn calming breathing exercises
- Take a long bath and unwind
- Use anything the home will provide, clothes, chair, TV, food, warmth

- Play calming and comforting music
- Do something physical to reduce stress hormones
- Spend time quietly thinking about a special place
- Do something nice for somebody else
- Read
- Think about all your good points – there are plenty
- Practice a relaxation exercise

Your clients can boost their self-esteem by making a permanent list of some of their good qualities to have in the home when they need it. It doesn't matter what goes on the list, as long as it's about them and it says something good then it will work.

A typical list might look something like this.

I am:
Honest
Funny
Independent
Proud of myself
Good at sport
Hard working
A good dancer
A tryer

This list will create more impact when it's needed if it's not a permanent fixture, then, on days when your clients might need a boost, they can prop it up where it can easily be seen.

Logging successes is another way to look after a fragile sense of self, this reinforces how well an individual is doing. Achievements can be written down, anything from remembering not to run out of milk to passing an important exam. If a client has been trying to achieve something and has succeeded, then it will be worthy of being logged. A notebook should be kept just for this purpose where the date can be filled in, what the success was and the feelings it created.

As time goes by there will be plenty of evidence of the successes in your clients' lives to reflect on when they need to.

3.4 Spread the happiness

Doing something to make another person happy is a certain way to make your clients feel happy themselves. Knowing you can make someone happy just by doing a small thing is very addictive – the more pleasure you get from it, the more you want to do it. Clients can use simple ways to create a happy atmosphere, from a simple smile or giving a compliment, to running an errand or sending a thoughtful message. If they are not in the habit of thinking this way, they might be surprised to learn the incredible fact that by making somebody else happy, all you feel is happiness yourself. It is good for them too, there is lots of scientific evidence to show how beneficial it is to perform kind acts towards other people.[10]

If your individuals like getting outside then going for a walk after dark can be very enjoyable. It is very different to going out in daylight and the general atmosphere can be incredibly soothing, even in a busy urban area, everything changes when the sun goes down. Rain shouldn't put them off either, getting wet and not worrying about it will create an attitude of

---

[10] *Why Kindness is Good For You*, p.225-227, David R. Hamilton

freedom and abandonment and can be a real boost.

It might be hard for your clients to maintain belief in their own abilities once the first novelty of independence has worn off. The work you do with them now on managing negative emotions will play a crucial part in achieving sustained success in their new homes.

One of the most important skills your clients can learn is how to use basic relaxation techniques. This will stand them in good stead whenever they begin to feel anxious or edgy. These techniques can be used at home as well as silently while out.

Below is a simple but effective relaxation technique you can teach your clients. It would be a good idea for you to experience this for yourself too, it doesn't involve anything except sitting on a comfortable chair or lying down on a bed or the floor.

Get comfortable and have the body in a straight line, not leaning too much to the left or right. Breathe in deeply, hold for a second or two then breathe out slowly, relax into the support.

Now just breathe naturally.

Think about the feet. The toes are still, feet are flopped outward.

Allow a feeling of relaxation to spread through the feet and into the legs, allow them to feel heavy and become aware of them being supported.

Allow this feeling of relaxation to spread to the hips and the pelvic area then up to the stomach and chest. Breathe evenly and calmly.

Be aware of the back, just allow the muscles of the back to relax.

Think about the hands, they are soft and relaxed with the fingers gently curling. Allow a feeling of relaxation to spread through the hands, the arms and into the shoulders. Allow them to feel heavy, try to relax the neck and throat.

Become aware of how heavy the head is and feel it being supported.

Think about the face, try not to clench the teeth or frown. Allow the tongue to relax in the mouth. The eyes are closed, the eyelids still. Imagine the forehead is high and wide and allow a feeling of relaxation to spread through the scalp.

Now become aware of the whole body, relaxed and feeling heavy. Just breathe gently and try to focus the mind on the breath.

Stay in this position for about five minutes then return the focus of the mind to the body, take a gentle stretch and come up slowly. If coming up from a lying position always turn on to one side for a few moments before coming right up.

To begin with, up to ten minutes is a good time to relax for; times can be adjusted later as your clients become used to it. Fifteen to twenty minutes is a good time to aim towards in order to feel real benefits.

If your clients find themselves getting anxious while they are out, they can learn to take a couple of deep breaths and then focus the mind on breathing calmly. A quick mental check through the shoulders, hands, neck and jaw will highlight any tension and this can then be focussed on and the areas relaxed.

Once learnt, this very simple technique can prevent feelings of anxiety from escalating and quickly restore a healthy balance.

3.5 Express Yourself!

It is crucial that your clients' ideas be allowed to flow naturally – you can encourage them to let their imaginations take control. When this happens they will soon start to experience the excitement that real inspiration can bring. Writing and drawing are excellent ways to start creating an outlet for their imagination.

Many people find that once they tap into their creative side they get the best out of it when they have more than one project on the go at a time. Creativity feeds creativity and your clients will find that as they gain confidence and ideas come to fruition, many more will be bubbling up inside just bursting to get out. They may also find that although they feel passionate about something, this might actually turn out to be a stepping stone on the way to something completely different. We never know where our imaginations will lead us but nothing is wasted and your clients' homes are where they can experiment with ideas freely, giving themselves complete autonomy and freedom of thought.

During your work on this subject you may find clients are a little inhibited to begin with when it comes to showing or sharing either their ideas or what they have created, and you may have to be willing to share some of your own work in order to break down barriers. Remember, if this does happen, that art work, whatever form it takes, is subjective, so don't be shy, everything you produce in this direction will be valid and worthy.

If individuals are not used to doing it, writing can feel quite a difficult thing to start and some people even feel a bit intimidated by the thought of it. However, you can help with overcoming these feelings and once this happens writing can be one of the most therapeutic forms of self-expression there is. There are no boundaries to where the imagination may go.

Writing can take many forms and your clients can be introduced to all of the ways below to see what appeals, there are no limitations and they might enjoy more than one.

- Keep a diary or journal, either on computer or in a notebook

- Write short stories

- Experiment with poems

- Create a catalogue of characters with backstories

- Write reviews of books, music or films. Expressing opinions this way helps with critical thinking skills.

- Write a book

- Write articles on anything of interest

- Write down general thoughts and observations on life

- Lists

- Letters, either on computer or by hand

As you can see, writing can be something factual and practical or something completely made up. Because creative writing comes from the imagination it is a route through to a fantasy world that could be difficult to access via any other medium. When your clients open their minds to it they will be able to get in touch with a rich source of ideas and images that can then be committed to the page.

Although all writing is a form of communication, there are two very different strands to it. Writing letters, texts and emails, and then things like stories or poems. Because texts and emails are so efficient and simple, these might be the only type of correspondence your clients use. However, the physical act of hand writing letters and putting them in the post can be both creative and satisfying.

Georgina Harris[11] states that letters 'are practical magic' and I'm sure we can all identify with the excitement of seeing a handwritten envelope drop through our door. However, it might be that your clients never write a letter by hand or receive one and, if this is the case, you can encourage them to acquire paper and pens and send a newsy letter to somebody. Choosing a way to present themselves through letter writing will provide another opportunity to express personality. A computer can be used to design an individual style for letter headings or freehand drawing is effective in decorating the paper and the envelopes. A big impact can be created when somebody receives a little of a client's personality through the post. Individuals may be surprised at how exciting it can be to anticipate a response and how imaginative other people are when they write back.

Writing by hand can be an art form in itself. From a simple form of calligraphy to the very intricate writings and illustrations of ancient texts, the act of actually composing the letters can be very complex.

Using the formation of letters for the purpose of creating a piece of art work is an interesting concept and if your clients are interested in following this up there are plenty of books showing how to go about it. However, for writing a personal letter handwriting is good enough or, if computers are preferred, this is fine too, it can then be printed off and posted.

Being able to write a personal letter will provide opportunities for your clients to look at various aspects of their lives. Their news needs to sound positive and interesting and when they can see things truthfully written down in this way, it provides evidence both to the receiver of the letter and also to the sender that life is going well. One of the benefits of writing an old-fashioned letter is that it allows for

---

[11] *The Art of Letter Writing*, p.7, Georgina Harris

expansion, for example, if an individual is in the middle of learning how to dismantle parts of a cycle or learning how to cook, in the normal course of texting or emailing something like this will not be spoken about in any depth. Through letter writing though, this is exactly what would be talked about, a client would be telling somebody what they are doing and why, and how they feel about it. This has the effect of affirming big chunks of their life and make them feel proud to be able to talk about them.

Sending letters and cards through the post opens up other opportunities that are not possible through electronic communication. For example, something can be enclosed in the envelope that will interest the receiver, maybe a small image of a large painting. If it is an affectionate letter then a piece of fabric or a flower might be appropriate. Sending messages to somebody this way provides so much more than just information, the recipient will have something tangible of the sender, something they can physically get hold of. Paper can easily be infused with smells and used this way, can evoke powerful memories. As well as all of this they can be kept safe and may well become valued treasures by the recipient.

There may also be times when your clients will want to write an angry letter. This can be done to vent feelings and then 'posted' into a cupboard or drawer. Writing this type of letter can be very therapeutic, it allows individuals to express emotion freely while feeling confident that there will be no repercussions. After a few weeks, when they read the letter again they will probably wonder what all the fuss was about and tear it up.

As with all the projects within my book, it will be up to each of your clients to decide how much they actually want to engage with. The idea is to introduce writing as a creative outlet, bringing out their original ideas and providing insight into who they really are. By introducing individuals to this while you are working with them, it will become second nature by the time they become independent.

Creative writing is an area with a different purpose and you can provide your clients with the motivation to get started. They may already have ideas in their heads so a writing journal is a good resource to have. You can encourage them to have it with them all the time to write down notes and ideas as they happen.

There are various techniques to help to get the imagination going.

Below is an excellent exercise Julia Bell provides to get anybody started.[12] It can be used with a group or with just one person.

Ask your clients to sit quietly for a few moments and just listen. Now, write down three sounds they can hear or three objects they can see around them. The sounds might be of birds, the wind, conversation, traffic, the objects might be books, clothes, cups, literally anything that can be seen or heard.

Next, write a list of what these things remind them of. For example, the sound of a bird may remind them of a walk or a garden, a person, a holiday. Whatever it is, they should write it down. Seeing a cup might make them think of when they last had coffee with somebody or when they visited somebody's house, or doing the washing up. All of these objects will have unique associations to them and the words written down will be the very start of a voice as a writer.

Another exercise you can use is one for a poem or piece of prose. This can be written any way a client chooses and they don't need to get bogged down with technicalities about the words, whatever is written is fine.

Ask your clients to write the words "Did I Ever Tell You"

---

[12] *The Creative Writing Coursebook*, Chpts 1-2, Eds. Julia Bell & Paul Magrs

at the top of the paper, then carry on writing whatever comes into their minds. It can be about anything or anybody. It can be real or made up, these are things for individuals to decide.

The point of introducing your clients to writing is that it is so versatile, it stretches the mind and the imagination and provides precious and special time out from everyday life.

As you work on this subject there are one or two simple practical things to consider. When writing clients will need to sit in a comfortable position with their materials around them. A table would be ideal but if this is not possible then something else which is firm enough to lean on, maybe a tray or a heavy book. They will also need a folder or box to keep their writing things together.

It is your job to enable the people you work with to develop the skills they will need to look after their own welfare when they are living alone. Boredom and apathy need to be kept at bay and creative activities are one of the best ways to achieve this. The home will be the one place where they can allow their imaginations to be free, the one place to feel at ease with inspirational ideas.

Drawing

Drawing is something that your clients may have been doing all their lives or, they may never have attempted it, thinking it is something they just can't do. Sometimes it can be quite difficult to put down on paper the images in our heads but, however it comes out, it will have value.

When I had a special birthday a few years back I asked all my grandchildren to draw me a picture. They were aged between three and five at the time and I have all their drawings framed and on a wall in my home. To me they are all abstract in design but when I talked to them about what they had produced they all had a clear idea of what the image was. It really doesn't matter what it looks like or means to another person, it is how your clients see it and what they feel when they are creating it that counts. As well as this, they will get a huge confidence boost if they then frame it and hang it on a wall.

Giving a drawing away as a gift is a very special thing to do too, and the recipient will feel very privileged at receiving such a thing.

If drawing or painting is something your clients are not used to doing then its best to keep it simple. Some plain lead or watercolour pencils and some paper is all they need to get started. They can go outside to find something interesting to draw or use something within the home. They could look into a mirror to do a self-portrait or study a photograph of a place or person. There are no rules or boundaries, and although a picture may start off as a known object or scene, it can easily evolve into something completely different.

This is an area that can build confidence very quickly; as pictures become formed and ideas move on they can be displayed around the home for further inspiration.

Talent is all in the eye of the beholder so your clients can take comfort in the knowledge that nobody will be in a position to judge the end results of their work. Drawing will be another tool individuals can use in the defence against negative emotions. If they are to succeed in running a home and a life then time needs to be filled constructively. It is your job to explore options open to all your clients and find a way that will enable them to express themselves freely.

3.6 Clothes

As we have already seen, creativity can be shown in many ways; many of us show it in the way we dress. Clothing is a way to make statements, rebel or conform, all by choosing what we wear. At any age it is possible to still be discovering personal identity. Clothing is an incredibly important outlet which can show individuality and flare.

There is evidence[13] to show that clothes can be a powerful way to reinforce and display an individual's characteristics. Things such as their innocence or sexuality, their confidence and also their political stances. Your clients can reveal, or indeed conceal their character by using clothes to their advantage, they can personalise ready-made clothing or they can try designing and making their own.

If you think back to your own experiences with clothing you may well remember a piece of statement clothing that you have owned and worn, and maybe still do. I know I can, and I can also remember how it made me feel. Like most people, when experimenting with different ideas my motivations around clothes have been very simple. I have wanted to appear to be on trend but different from the crowd. I can remember buying fabric on a Saturday morning, cutting and sewing it into a dress during the afternoon and wearing it out in the evening. It really was that simple, it might not have had a top designer label on but it was my design. I was always bursting with ideas and enthusiasm about how I wanted my clothes to look and couldn't wait to add bits of my own to tweak items I had bought to make them different from everyone else's. I believe a lot of my enthusiasm was coming from the fact that I was still discovering my real identity as an individual, and during this time was full of energy and ideas with some strong feelings about pursuing how I thought I wanted to look and appear to other people.

I believe this is a fairly typical outlook for anybody still working out their individuality and the people you work with

---

[13] *Understanding Youth: Perspectives, Identities and Practices*, p.267, Ed. Mary Jane Kehily

have opportunities to experiment with ideas around image with the benefit of your input. It is incredibly important that clients feel comfortable with how they look and in control of how other people see them.

Although the start might be tentative, using clothes as a tool to promote individuality and help establish identity will help strengthen character and help in avoiding falling victim to the fashion corporations of the day. Only when your clients begin to understand how clothes can make them feel can they start to be clear about how to achieve a way of dressing that fits with who they are and the life they lead.

What an individual wears will have a direct impact on how they feel. Whether it's a day lounging around at home or a special night out, our clothes can have a bearing on our mood and our motivation. It would be good for you to spend time with your clients experimenting with the clothes they own. Encourage them to try things on, this way they can really think about how different items make them feel. This exercise will help to develop a way of dressing that suits individual personalities. It will allow each person to express their true nature as well as allowing them to make a statement if they want to or to keep things private if they prefer.

There are various ways you can tap into inspirational ideas around styles and fabrics for clothes, use the suggestions below and have discussions with your clients. Encourage them to visit some of the places and to write down their ideas. This will all help them to get started on this important self-affirming work.

- Look closely at anybody you admire and notice what they are wearing.

- Films – these show wide-ranging styles, colours and fabrics. Look with new eyes and make a note of anything really appealing.

- History is peppered with all sorts of fashion and style concepts; images are accessible through the internet or books and the key is to look only at the clothes, just let everything else go.

- Other cultures can be inspirational, producing very different styles and finishes, all adding to the mix of what can be said through garments.

- Art galleries and museums can often show fantastic clothing made from fabric which is rich in colour and texture such as velvet or tapestry, right down to exquisitely worked sheer fabrics such as voile. These places can provide so much inspiration and if something really appeals to your clients, with a little effort, it wouldn't be too difficult to reproduce it in something wearable. For example, a female might like the style of a medieval velvet dress, this could be transformed into a warm velvet tunic to wear over tight jeans.

- Looking at different lifestyles can open up opportunities for ideas as these show clothes worn for different occasions, for example walking or outdoor clothes have a specific look to them, similarly with sport or office wear.

It is your job to explore with your clients just how much of themselves they want to put into their clothes and how they feel about revealing their personalities to the world in this way. Below are some questions you can use to initiate discussions around the issue. Remember though, that if they prefer to reveal nothing at all in this way, this is fine too.

- Do you want to look like somebody in particular?

- Would you want people to know the job you do or the training or college you attend?

- Do you want to be the same as your peers?

- Do you like to be seen as an individual?

- Do you think your financial status should be reflected in your clothes?

- Would you want to show the label of your clothing, if so, why?

By gradually working through some of these questions your clients will start to get a clearer picture of how they would like the world to see them, this in turn will help them to recognise how they see themselves. When we are comfortable with the way we look and how we are perceived by the people around us, it removes enormous tensions from our lives and builds self-esteem.

Clothes are a statement to the world and through our clothes we can control what people think of us. Manufacturers of designer label clothing make massive amounts of money by tapping into our desire to be recognised in a certain way. Your clients can tap into their own creative resources and be recognised as an individual whose ideas on clothing should be taken seriously, showing the world how proud they are to be exactly who they are right now.

Once this starts to happen their confidence will soar and they will be amazed as they start to recognise their own potential.

3.7 Something to give

Giving, from your clients' perspectives, might be seen as something only wealthy or time-rich individuals can afford to do, and this is probably not how they see themselves. However, to prepare for long hours of being alone, now is the time for you to sow inspirational seeds that will shake up ideas on how or what they can give to make a difference.

It is likely that the people you work with may see themselves as having less than most and that they have very little of value to give to anyone. You can challenge this belief and show that they have so much to offer that they can afford to dig deep into themselves and give freely. Your clients can learn that when they give, they will receive, probably more than they would expect. The experience of this can have a big impact, enhancing their lives and adding significantly to their sense of well-being.

Giving can be done on many different levels and to get your clients thinking about it in a realistic way you can introduce the idea that giving doesn't have to cost anything except a little time here and there. It doesn't have to be all about the big things, small gestures will still have a huge impact on your clients' lives and reduce the chances of problems arising as they try to maintain independent life successfully. However, they may find that because the rewards are so great they will want to do it more and more, if this happens they can look around for something they really enjoy and make a fuller commitment.

Giving free time is a brilliant way to get started. They will need to be open, flexible and creative, being guided by their instincts about what they do. You can help by looking at various options so that when independent, your clients will have knowledge and experience to rely on, thus providing the confidence to spread their wings a little. Gradually, as more opportunities begin to open up, individuals will experience the good feelings that only come from genuinely giving something from within.

To start work on this subject you will need to have discussions with your clients about their interests and what appeals. This might involve something they feel very passionate about and can be used as a stepping stone into an area of possible work or a fuller commitment, or it might be something very simple like helping a friend out every now and again. It doesn't matter what it is, every time they do it, the rewards will be the same.

On a small and manageable scale there are lots of options to consider and you can use the suggestions below to promote thinking.

Offer help to a more vulnerable person, perhaps someone who lives close by or who attends the same college or place of work

Help a friend with chores

Run an errand

Go shopping with somebody

Cook someone a meal

Help somebody choose clothes

Open the door for somebody

Be the one to clear the dishes

Help somebody to read

Take time to listen

All of these things are about giving small amounts of time and energy, they don't even have to be done on a regular basis so there's no need for commitment. However, there are plenty of opportunities for clients to formalise their giving if they should want to. Many organisations use volunteers and without this kind of help, many of them would cease to exist. Use the list below to create discussions about their interests.

Marketing

Retail

Animals

Outdoor, countryside

Administration

Fundraising

All of these things can be applied to a variety of organisations. For example, an individual might like to work with animals, volunteering would introduce them to many aspects of the job. Apart from working hands-on, there would be opportunities to help with fundraising, marketing, selling directly to the public as well as other administrative tasks. By spreading themselves around their chosen field and learning about the different aspects involved, they will develop all kinds of transferrable skills as well as gain insight into the whole nature of the work.

Some large charitable organisations work all over the world providing basic things like water and healthcare. Although the front line might not be the place to start, individuals can be part of what is going on by offering a few hours a week in a shop that supports this cause. Here they will learn a lot about the practicalities of what goes on in the organisation as well as provide the satisfaction of supporting something they really believe in.

This very tentative start with giving freely may well inspire your clients to think about longer-term goals and ambitions. Volunteering provides such scope for experiencing life in ways that most of us could never achieve in our normal lifestyles. For example, if there is a passion for wildlife an individual can set their sights on working abroad with elephants for a year.

There are no boundaries to what your clients can aim for and any experience gained by working like this on a small scale will be taken into account when the time comes to commit to something bigger. Giving time is also taken seriously when it comes to college or job applications and will be a valuable addition to any C.V.

The benefits of giving free time are enormous and something everybody should be able to experience. The list below shows some of them.

Relieves boredom and stress

Provides opportunities to make new friends

Teaches new skills

Can lead to employment

Builds confidence and self esteem

Creates a sense of being needed

Provides job satisfaction

Brings out the passion

Provides fun

Expands the mind and opens up unplanned possibilities

There are lots of books and websites providing information on volunteering for anybody interested and it can be done with a variety of approaches.

Giving can be done on a practical basis to the needy or to a charity, this would mean giving cash or useful items.

Teaching somebody how to do something is an incredibly valuable way of giving and although your clients may not realise it, they have the skills to teach something. It might be riding a bike, playing a board game or teaching somebody to read, they can do it.

Then there is helping somebody directly in order for them to achieve their end goal. This might be in any area of life at any time and the scope is endless, from helping somebody pass an exam to carrying a heavy shopping bag.

Adopting the mind set of giving freely will change your clients' perspectives on how they see themselves. Their lives will be enhanced both within the home and outside it, creating a stabilising effect and a sense of purpose.

The most important thing to understand is that everyone has the capability to give. Your clients have much more inside them than they probably realise and the potential to discover this is locked into experiencing what it feels like to be the provider instead of the receiver.

And Finally…

Through my book it has been my aim to show practical ways to help individuals, who may have had a potentially chaotic start to life, give themselves a real chance to succeed with living independently. I hope I have also shown how crucial your role is, as a Carer or Support Worker, in this success.

As we have seen, success depends on many different factors including the clients' personalities and determination. However, as we have also seen, with enough support and encouragement it is possible that a lot of the factors that are involved in success can be learned or changed.

My hope is that after going through my book, your clients will learn that they can be proud to own their own histories. I hope too that they will be strong enough to trust their own memories and feelings and have greater awareness of the validity of these. This will enable them to reach an understanding that these can be built on with confidence, thus providing the foundations, inspirations and sense of belonging that will support them in their move on to the future.

ABOUT THE AUTHOR

Eileen Williams has been a foster carer, worked at a project for homeless young people and also with ex-offenders living in a probation hostel.

Eileen's qualifications include B.A. Hons. Literary/ Cultural Studies, Diploma in Counselling Skills, NVQ Advice and Guidance, Diploma in Creative Writing, C & G Further and Adult Education Teachers Certificate, British Wheel of Yoga Diploma, Diploma in Teaching Meditation.

Printed in Great Britain
by Amazon